CONTENTS

MP3467/Inside Judaism © Milliken Publishing Company

 AN OVERVIEW OF JUDAISM

Of the world's five major religions, Judaism claims the fewest followers. There are only about 13 million people of the Jewish faith spread throughout the world. In the year 2011, Christianity had the most followers, followed by Islam, Hinduism, and Buddhism. Even a number of lesser-known religions boast more converts than Judaism. Yet it is from Judaism that the world's two largest religions—Christianity and Islam—sprang.

Judaism is one of the oldest organized religions in the world. It traces its beginnings back some 4,000 years to Abraham, who is called the "Father of the Hebrews." Judaism is the first religion to practice monotheism, or the belief in one god. Jews, as the followers of Judaism are called, refer to God as Yahweh.

Throughout much of their history, the Jews have been persecuted by other peoples and nations. For nearly 2000 years after the fall of the ancient Jewish kingdoms of Israel and Judah, Jews were scattered throughout the world, unable to realize their dream of a homeland until 1948. Yet during the long interval, they managed to keep their identity. While they may have adopted the language and some of the customs of other countries, they have always clung to their religion and way of life.

What strong bonds have kept the Jewish people together through centuries of trial and uncertainty? Why did some ancient religions fade away, while Judaism prevailed? You will find answers to these and other questions as you read *Inside Judaism*. You will also learn about Jewish beliefs, customs, ceremonies, and other aspects of Jewish religion and life. Finally, you will learn about and gain an appreciation for the enormous contributions of the Jewish people to the culture and history of the world, not least of which are the Ten Commandments and the Old Testament.

CHAPTER ONE

Early Jewish History

The early history of the Jewish people took place in what is now the state of Israel. In those days, however, this land, located on the eastern shore of the Mediterranean Sea, was called Canaan. Much later it became known as Palestine. When a Jewish homeland was established there in 1948, it was thereafter called Israel.

But we are far ahead of our story. The Jewish people, or Hebrews as they were called long ago, did not migrate into Canaan until sometime between 2100 and 1500 B.C. Until then, their ancestors lived in Mesopotamia. Mesopotamia was a large region located in what is now the Middle East. (Today, much of the region makes up the modern nation of Iraq.) It was situated between two mighty rivers—the Tigris and the Euphrates— and its name means "land between the rivers." It is here that our story of Jewish history begins about 4,000 years ago.

Abraham

As stated in the overview, Jewish history begins with Abraham. Abraham was the patriarch, or head, of his tribe. A tribe is a group of people descended from a common ancestor. In short, a tribe is like one big family. But what a family! In Abraham's time, households were very large, with sons and their wives and children living at home, along with those son's sons and their wives and offspring and so on.

Abraham had many responsibilities. As head of his tribe, he had a hand in everything. He settled disputes and punished lawbreakers. He officiated at religious ceremonies, saying prayers and offering sacrifices at the altar. He led his tribe into wars with other tribes.

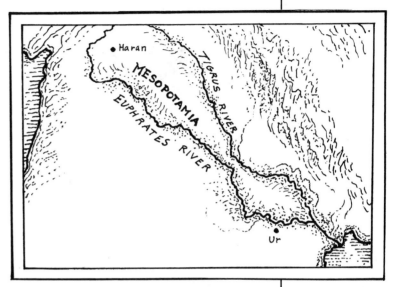

Perhaps Abraham's greatest responsibility was to look after the well-being of his tribe. Because they were goatherds and shepherds, Abraham decided where they would live. If there was not sufficient water and grass in one area, the tribe moved to another. Thus it was that Abraham left the region around Ur in Mesopotamia and moved his tribe to Haran. Haran was an ancient city to the northwest, approximately 600 miles from Ur. Today it is part of southeast Turkey.

It was at Haran that God is said to have revealed himself to Abraham. It was also at Haran that Jews (and Christians) believe God gave Abraham the following instructions, as recorded in Genesis 12:1 of the Old Testament:

Now the Lord had said unto Abram (as Abraham was known in those days), *"Get thee out of thy country, and from thy kindred, and from thy father's house, unto a land that I will shew thee."*

Even though Abraham was 75 years old at the time, he was not about to disobey God. According to Judaism, God had made a covenant with Abraham that

---

Jewish history begins with Abraham who left the city of Ur in Mesopotamia and moved his tribe to the northern city of Haran. It was at Haran that God is said to have revealed himself to Abraham saying, "Get thee out of thy country, and from thy kindred, and from thy father's house, unto a land that I will shew thee."

Words to remember:

Canaan
Mesopotamia
Abraham
Haran
Ur

he would give Abraham's descendants the land of Canaan as their home if they carried out God's will. The covenant became a contract between Abraham's followers and God. As long as they served God and obeyed him, they

Although Abraham's father was an idol merchant, Abraham believed in one god who created the earth and everything on it.

Words to remember:

Terah
Yahweh
Isaac
Mount Moriah

would be God's Chosen People. Knowing this, Abraham gathered his family and followers together and departed for the land of Canaan.

Canaan was a narrow strip of land about 600 miles to the south. It was only 130 kilometers (81 miles) wide at its broadest point. Length-wise, it measured about 241 kilometers, or 150 miles. It was bordered on the west by the Mediterranean Sea, on the east by the Arabian Desert, on the south by Egypt, and on the north by Mesopotamia. To this land Abraham led his tribe.

Section Review:

1. What is a tribe?
2. To where did Abraham move when he left the city of Ur? Why did he and his family feel the necessity to relocate?
3. What covenant do Jews believe God made with Abraham?
4. Where was the land of Canaan?

Two Intriguing Stories

No one in Jewish history is more loved and respected than Abraham. Jewish lore is filled with countless stories about the great patriarch. One of the most interesting stories concerns an incident that took place when Abraham was a boy living in his father's house in Ur. His father, Terah, was an idol merchant, and because everyone in those days worshiped idols, business was good. But Abraham wasn't all that interested in idols. He had, in fact, slowly come to regard idol worship as a waste of time. In his mind he had formulated the image of one god, a god who was the creator of the earth and everything on it.

One day when Terah was out of the shop, Abraham took a hammer and smashed all the idols except the largest one. In the hands of this large statue he placed the hammer. When his father returned and stood aghast at the damage, Abraham is believed to have said, "Father, while you were gone, the idols got into a fight. The big one who is now holding the hammer won."

"That's ridiculous," his father retorted. "Idols can't think. Idols have no will of their own. Idols have no power. They are incapable of doing anything."

"Then why do you worship them?" Abraham asked, no doubt with a certain smugness in his voice.

Another story is more familiar. It deals with God ordering Abraham to sacrifice his young son, Isaac, on an altar. In those days, it was common practice to sacrifice a human being to the gods. According to Hebrew tradition, God, or Yahweh as the early Jews referred to him, decided to test Abraham's faith by commanding him to offer Isaac as a sacrifice. Abraham, although disheartened at the thought of his son dying, was determined to carry out God's will.

The sacrifice was to take place atop a mountain called Mount Moriah. The mountain was three days journey from Abraham's home. Abraham made the journey with two servants and his son Isaac. Isaac, of course, had no idea he was to be the "sacrificial lamb." He was, in fact, very excited that his father asked him to come along and help carry wood for the sacrificial fire.

When Abraham and his party reached the top of Mount Moriah, he ordered Isaac to place the wood on top of a rock suitable to serve as an altar. Then he bound his son's hands and feet and prepared to plunge a knife into him. Who knows what thoughts must have raced through Isaac's mind as he realized his father was going to kill him? Abraham, despite tears streaming down his face, raised the knife and prepared to carry out God's instructions. Just then God is said to have called out (Genesis 22: 11-12): "Abraham, Abraham!" And Abraham replied, "Here am I." God said, "Do not lay your hand on the lad or do anything to him; for now I know that you fear God, seeing you have not withheld your son, your only son, from me."

At the same moment, Abraham and Isaac heard a rustle in a nearby bush. A ram had gotten caught in the thorns of the bush and was unable to escape. The ancient Hebrews believed that God had provided the ram to serve as the sacrifice. This done, Abraham and his son descended Mount Moriah and went home.

Section Review:

1. Why did Abraham smash the idols in his father's shop?
2. Why did God order Abraham to sacrifice his only son on Mount Moriah?
3. What did Abraham's willingness to slay his son say about his relationship with God?

Moses

After a while, a famine forced the Hebrews to leave Canaan and go to Egypt. Some, who came to be called Israelites, had gone there earlier. There they lived in peace for some time, prospering in a part of Egypt called the

God tested Abraham by asking him to sacrifice his only son.

**Moses
Land of Goshen
Pentateuch**

According to Jewish tradition, God appeared to Moses in the form of a burning bush and instructed him to return to Egypt and lead the Hebrews out of captivity.

"Land of Goshen." After about 400 years, however, they were made slaves by the Egyptians, and remained in bondage for several centuries.

Enter Moses, the second great leader of the ancient Hebrews. His story is told in the Bible in the books of Exodus, Leviticus, Numbers, and Deuteronomy. These books, along with Genesis, are referred to as the Pentateuch, or the Books of Moses. *Pentateuch*, in Greek, means "five books."

Moses was born in Egypt sometime in the 13th century B.C. It was not a good time to be born, for the Pharaoh, or king, of Egypt had decreed that every son born of a Hebrew woman should be cast into the Nile River. The Pharaoh believed that the Hebrews had grown in such numbers that they posed a threat to his regime. His order to kill all male babies was an attempt to reduce the Hebrew population.

Yocheved, Moses' mother, hid him for several months in her home. Then she put him in a basket along the banks of the Nile River, hoping for the best. Luckily, he was found by a daughter of the Pharaoh, who took him home to her father's palace and raised him as her son.

Moses grew up to be a prince. He learned to read and write, and he became quite important at court. However, something happened that caused him to have to leave Egypt. One day he saw an Egyptian official severely beating a Hebrew. He came to the Hebrew's defense, and in the process of defending him, killed the Egyptian. To save his life, Moses was forced to flee. He went to the land of Midian, which was located east of the northern tip of the Red Sea. There he lived among the Midianites. He married, had two children, and lived the life of a shepherd for 40 years.

One day while Moses was tending his father-in-law's flock, God is said to have appeared to him in the form of a burning bush. The ancient Hebrews believed that as Moses stood dumbfounded, God gave him instructions to return to Egypt and lead the Hebrews (who, for the sake of simplicity, we shall henceforth refer to as the Israelites) out of captivity. Although Moses was a little reluctant, he knew he had to obey God's command.

Moses left Midian and returned to Egypt. Because he had a problem with his speech (he stammered), he asked his brother Aaron to speak for him when they went to see the Pharaoh. They asked the Pharaoh to free the Israelites and to allow them to return to Canaan. The Pharaoh refused. The book of Exodus then states that God sent ten plagues to punish Egypt. These plagues ranged from turning the waters into blood to flooding the land with flies and locusts. But the Pharaoh held firm until the tenth plague, which was by far the worst.

As revealed in Exodus 11: 4–7 and 12: 29–30, the tenth plague had the Angel of Death visit each Egyptian home and take the life of the first-born child. Even the Pharaoh's first-born child was not spared.

The angel, however, passed over the houses of the Israelites and did not harm their first-born children. (Jews today celebrate this event as the Passover, which they refer to as Pesach. The name also refers to the Exodus, or the passing over of the Israelites from slavery to freedom. You will learn more about Pesach in Chapter Seven.)

When his own son was taken from him, Pharaoh Rameses II relented and agreed to let the Israelites go.

Section Review:

1. What is the Pentateuch?
2. What did the Israelites believe God instructed Moses to do?
3. Explain the origin of the term "Passover."
4. What finally convinced the Pharaoh to set the Israelites free?

The Exodus

Once the Israelites were free and on their way to the Land of Canaan, Rameses II went back on his word. He sent his army to overtake his former slaves and bring them back to captivity. His chariots and soldiers caught up with the Israelites and their cattle and sheep near the Red Sea. When this happened, Moses' followers looked back at the approaching Egyptians and cried that they were doomed. But then a miracle happened. According to Hebrew tradition, Moses lifted his staff and the sea parted, leaving a dry path in the middle that beckoned the Israelites to cross. They did, and when the Egyptians tried to follow, the sea closed again, drowning all of them.

This flight of the Israelites from Egypt is called the Exodus, meaning "a going out." It was to continue for forty years, although Moses and his followers had no idea at the time that such would be the case. At the moment, they were ecstatic that they had escaped the pursuing Egyptian army and were on

their way to the Promised Land.

Soon the journey through the wilderness became one of hardship. The Israelites constantly complained to

Moses about the shortage of food and water, and many openly confessed that they wished they had stayed in Egypt. Despite their complaints, Hebrew tradition states that God provided for their care. He sent food from Heaven in the form of manna, which was said to taste something like a wafer made with honey. And once, when the Israelites complained that the water at a certain place was undrinkable, God is said to have made it potable by instructing Moses to throw a log into it. When he

According to Hebrew tradition, when Rameses II caught up with the fleeing Israelites at the Red Sea, Moses lifted his staff and the sea parted, allowing his people safe passage. When the Egyptians tried to follow, the sea closed again, drowning all of them.

did, the water became sweet and pure.

After three months, the Israelites reached the foot of Mount Sinai, which is located on a peninsula at the two north arms of the Red Sea. It was here that Moses is said to have received the Ten Commandments from God. The ancient Hebrews believed he was summoned to the top of the mountain, where he stayed for forty days, conversing with God about the commandments and other matters. During his absence, the Israelites got tired of waiting and regressed back to their Egyptian days of idol worship. They melted down their jewelry and created a golden calf to which they offered sacrifices at an altar they had built before it.

When Moses at last came down from the mountain, he was shocked at what he saw. He found his people not only worshipping a golden idol but drinking, brawling, and dancing as well. They had cast aside God's commandments and were indulging in every imaginable pleasure. Moses was furious.

If Moses was furious, you can imagine God's mood. To punish the Israelites for their behavior and actions, the book of Exodus states that God condemned them to wander in the wilderness for 40 years. None of those who left Egypt with Moses were ever to see the Promised Land. Only their children would be allowed to enjoy the fruits of the "Land of Milk and Honey." Even Moses himself was denied entry into Canaan. God granted him only a glimpse of the land from atop Mount Nemo. Shortly thereafter, at age 120, he died.

Section Review:

1. What name is given to the Israelites' flight from Egypt?
2. Where is Moses said to have received the Ten Commandments from God?
3. How do Jews believe God punished the Israelites for falling back into idol worship?

Upon reaching the foot of Mount Sinai, the ancient Hebrews believed Moses was summoned by God to the top of the mountain where he is said to have stayed for 40 days. When he returned bearing the Ten Commandments, he found the Israelites engaged in idol worship and indulging in every imaginable pleasure. For this, God is said to have condemned them to wander in the the wilderness for 40 years.

Three Kings, Followed by Two Kingdoms

After forty years in the wilderness, the Israelites finally reached Canaan. Dates vary from source to source, but they seemed to have arrived sometime around 1200 B.C. For almost 200 years, from 1200 B.C. to 1020 B.C., the Israelites were ruled by officials called judges. A judge governed each of the loosely organized twelve tribes. However, because they were surrounded on all sides by stronger enemies, the Israelites realized they would have to unite if they wanted to survive. In 1020 B.C., they ended what is called the Period of Judges and formed the Kingdom of Israel, with Saul as its first king.

Saul ruled for 20 years. Although he fought successfully against such enemies as the Ammonites, Moabites, and Philistines, he lacked the wisdom the Israelites expected of their king. In 1000 B.C., he was defeated in a battle with the Philistines, as a result of which he killed himself by falling on his sword.

The Israelites chose David to be their next king. David had already made a name for himself when, armed with only a slingshot, he slew the Philistine giant Goliath. David was a much-loved king who established Jerusalem as the capital of his kingdom. He ruled from 1000 B.C. to 961 B.C.

David's son Solomon succeeded him to the throne. Solomon built the great Temple of Jerusalem, as well as roads, fortresses, and other structures that made Israel strong. More than anything, Solomon was known for his great wisdom. He was also noted for his extravagant use of the taxpayers' money. He had a harem of some 1000 wives and concubines, as well as a large number of expensive stables to house his multitude of horses. When he died in 922 B.C., after a reign of 39 years, Israel was ripe for revolt.

In the year Solomon died, the Israelites did in fact rebel. They split into two kingdoms: the Kingdom of Israel in the north and the Kingdom of Judah in the south. Their splitting into two nations led to their downfall, for neither kingdom was strong enough to beat back attacks by powerful empires that had formed in the region.

Section Review:

1. How were the Israelites ruled before they united and chose a king?
2. Which king made Jerusalem the capital of Israel?
3. How did Solomon's extravagance hasten the downfall of his kingdom?

David's son Solomon built the Temple of Jerusalem, as well as roads, fortresses, and other structures that made Israel strong.

Conquest and Captivity

As has already been mentioned, the Israelites were surrounded by other peoples from the start. All sought control of a fertile region that extended in an arc from the eastern end of the Mediterranean Sea to the Persian Gulf. Much of Mesopotamia lay within this area, which is known as the Fertile Crescent.

As long as the peoples and kingdoms that surrounded Israel were small, the Israelites managed to hold their own against their neighbors. But soon powerful empires appeared that threatened their existence. Three of these were the empires of the Assyrians, the Chaldeans, and the Persians.

In 722 B.C., Israel, the northern Jewish kingdom, was overrun by the Assyrians. The Assyrians were a warlike people known for their extreme cruelty. They tortured captured prisoners by flaying, or skinning, them alive. They destroyed the northern kingdom's capital (Samaria) and carried away many of the Israelites into captivity and slavery. These exiles in time came to be known as the Ten Lost Tribes of Israel. What really happened to them? There are many theories. Some historians maintain that they were gradually absorbed into the cultures of other Mesopotamian peoples. Other theories are not as believable. One states that the Lost Tribes found their way to the British Isles and that the people who live there today are their descendants. Another holds that the American Indians are direct descendants of these wayward Israelites.

The southern Israelite kingdom of Judah lasted much longer. But in time it too fell. In 586 B.C., the Chaldeans, whose capital was at Babylon on the Euphrates River, captured Judah. They destroyed the Temple built by Solomon in Jerusalem and carried the people away into slavery. Later, when the Chaldeans themselves were conquered by the Persians, the Persians permitted the people of Judah to return. The Israelites rebuilt their Temple, but they again found themselves dispersed when the Romans took over Palestine in the first century B.C.

After the fall of the kingdoms of Israel and Judah, the Jews remained scattered throughout the world until the formation of the modern state of Israel in 1948. That they were able to maintain their separate identity and religion during all those years attests to their courage and determination.

Section Review:

1. Where is the Fertile Crescent?
2. How did the people of the northern Jewish kingdom come to be called the "Ten Lost Tribes"?
3. Which people conquered the Kingdom of Judah?
4. When was the modern nation of Israel established?

For Further Thought:

1. Why is the study of Jewish history important?
2. How are families different today than they were in Abraham's time?
3. What do you think it meant when Abraham and his followers, through their covenant with God, became the "Chosen People"? If you had been told that you were "chosen," how might that make you feel? How might it shape your life?
4. Imagine yourself a Hebrew boy or girl living in captivity in ancient Egypt. Write a letter to Pharaoh Rameses II giving reasons why he should set your people free.
5. Create a dialogue between two of Moses' followers as they complain of their lot while wandering through the wilderness.
6. Compare the government in Israel during the Period of Judges with that of the United States under the Articles of Confederation. What problems are inherent in such a system?
7. What do you think happened to the Ten Lost Tribes of Israel? Give reasons for the conclusion you have drawn.
8. How might history have been different if the Israelite tribes had not separated into two kingdoms?

CHAPTER TWO
Great Hebrew Prophets

No study of early Jewish history is complete without a look at the role played by some of the Biblical prophets. From Amos to Malachi, the prophets guided the Israelites through troubled times and taught them the ways of their God.

Some people equate prophets with soothsayers. This is not necessarily so. *Prophet* is a word derived from a Greek word that means "one who proclaims." And that is exactly what the ancient prophets did. They did not predict the future as much as they proclaimed to the Israelites what might happen to them if they disobeyed God and ignored his commandments.

All told, there were somewhere between 15 and 20 ancient Hebrew prophets. Three are known as the Major Prophets. They are Isaiah, Jeremiah, and Ezekiel. Twelve comprise the category of the Minor Prophets. They are Hosea, Amos, Joel, Micah, Jonah, Obadiah, Nahum, Haggai, Habakkuk, Zephaniah, Zacariah, and Malachi. The writings of these prophets make up 15 books of the Old Testament. Three prophets, Elijah, Elisha, and Nathan, were so busy with the kings of Israel and Judah that they did not write anything.

Because of limited space, only some of the more important prophets are addressed in this chapter.

Amos

Amos was a shepherd who lived in Tekoa in the southern kingdom of Judah. But his concern was for the northern kingdom of Israel. Its people had gotten away from God's commandments, and its king, Jeroboam II, cared little for the sufferings of the poor. Around 750 or 740 B.C., Amos warned Jeroboam that Israel would fall if it didn't change its ways. His prophecy came true in 722 B.C. when the Assyrians conquered the kingdom. Amos was the first to see God as the universal god of all nations.

Hosea

Hosea lived about the same time as Amos. He was born in approximately 784 B.C. and died in 725 B.C. He too warned King Jeroboam that calamity would befall Israel if it didn't change its ways. He pointed to idol worship and the callousness of the people as leading to Israel's downfall. The central theme of Hosea's teachings was love. He encouraged the Israelites to show their love for God not through sacrifices but through kindness, fairness, and honesty. He compared God to a loving father who forgives his errant children.

Isaiah

There may have been two or three prophets named Isaiah. The one with whom we are concerned was born about 740 B.C. and died in 681 B.C. He lived at a time when Judah—the southern Israelite kingdom—was threatened by many conquerors. As did Amos and Hosea in the northern kingdom of Israel, Isaiah tried to make the people of the kingdom of Judah understand that they were being punished for their sins. He scolded them for thinking that because they believed they were God's Chosen People, they could behave in any manner they wished. He told them that because they had known God before any other peoples, more was expected of them.

Micah

Micah was a peasant who lived in Moreshet in Judah. He lived from about 730 B.C. to 705 B.C. Like the other prophets, he criticized the Israelites for their corruption and injustice. He predicted that Jerusalem would be conquered and the Temple destroyed. Micah pointed out the heart of the Jewish religion when he wrote in the eighth verse of the sixth chapter of his book: "...and what doth the Lord require of thee, but to do justly, and to love mercy, and to walk humbly with thy God."

Jeremiah

Jeremiah also predicted the destruction of Jerusalem and lived to see it.

Jeremiah was born in Anathoth in Judah about 650 B.C. His prophecy about Jerusalem's impending doom made him unpopular. People tried to kill him, and he was even put in prison. As he predicted, King Nebuchadnezzar of the Chaldean Empire conquered Judah and destroyed Jerusalem in 586 B.C. Most of the Jewish inhabitants were carried away as slaves, beginning a period of Jewish history called the Babylonian Captivity. While some sources say that Nebuchadnezzar permitted Jeremiah to stay in Jerusalem after the city's fall, others maintain that he too was carried away and that he died in exile in Babylon.

Malachi

We include Malachi because if Amos is considered by some to be the first prophet, Malachi was the last.

Because the name *Malachi* means "my messenger," this may not have been the real name of the last biblical prophet and author of the last book in the Old Testament. Regardless, he lived about the middle of the 5th century B.C. This was some 50 years after the exiles to Babylon had returned and rebuilt the Temple. Malachi emphasized that God was universal and that all people have worth. His book prophesied the coming of the Messiah.

Section Review:

1. How were the prophets different from soothsayers who predicted the future?
2. What people conquered the kingdom of Israel, therefore fulfilling the prophecy of Amos?
3. Which prophet predicted the downfall of the kingdom of Judah more than a hundred years before it occurred?
4. Which king conquered Jerusalem and destroyed the Temple?
5. Who was the last of the prophets?

Words to remember:

prophet
soothsayer
Amos
Jeroboam II
Hosea
Isaiah
Micah
Jeremiah
Malachi

King
Nebuchadnezzar

Babylonian
Captivity

For Further Thought:

1. What common theme ran through the warnings of the prophets to the peoples of the kingdoms of Israel and Judah?
2. Research and write a short paper on the life of one of the prophets mentioned in this chapter.
3. What personal traits do you think characterized the prophets of biblical times?
4. Why do you think God used prophets to convey his will to his people?
5. Pretend that newspapers existed in ancient times and that you are a reporter for *The Babylon Daily News*. Write a short article based on an interview you had with the prophet Jeremiah after the conquest of Judah by the Chaldeans.

11   MP3467/*Inside Judaism* © Milliken Publishing Company

Chapter Three

Since Ancient Times

After the fall of the kingdoms of Israel and Judah, the story of the Jews is one of wandering and persecution. After their expulsion from Judah during the Roman period, the Jews would not return to their homeland for almost two thousand years. They scattered throughout the world, settling in such places as Egypt and Greece, and later in France, Germany, England, Central Europe, Poland, and Russia. They considered themselves living in exile, during a period referred to as the *Diaspora* from the Greek word meaning "dispersal." During this long period, Jews kept their religion strong by emphasizing home life and family ties.

The Jews who migrated to Europe were generally left alone for hundreds of years. Their communities were rarely subjected to danger and they mingled freely with peoples of other faiths and backgrounds. Then came the Crusades, and Jewish life in Europe was never the same.

The First Crusade

In 622, a rival religion to Judaism and Christianity arose in Arabia. This religion was Islam. Its founder, Mohammed, preached that it was the duty of Muslims, as Mohammed's followers were called, to spread the new faith through "holy wars." Thus it was that the hallowed city of Jerusalem and the whole Fertile Crescent came under Arab control.

For almost 400 years, Christians from Europe who desired to go on pilgrimages to Jerusalem were not bothered by the Muslims. They were permitted to come and go as they pleased. All this changed, however, in the 11th century. In 1071, the Turks, a less-tolerant group of

Muslims, conquered Jerusalem. They made the holy city part of their Ottoman Empire, and immediately began to make things difficult for Christian pilgrims. Travelers who sought to enter the land of the Turks had to pay a high tax to do so. Worse, they were often cruelly mistreated. All this led to a call by Pope Urban II for a Crusade to free the Holy Land from the Muslims.

You may be wondering what the struggle between Christian Europe and the Ottoman Turks had to do with the Jews. The explanation lies in the fact that many Christians blamed the Jews for the death of Christ. Since they considered the Jews to be infidels like the Muslims (as Jews did not accept the divinity of Christ), the Crusades afforded an opportunity to wipe out Jewish populations that were located along the path to Jerusalem.

In 1095, the First Crusade set out. Along the way, in Jewish communities situated on the Rhine and Danube Rivers, the Crusaders slaughtered innocent and helpless Jews by the thousands. In Worms, Germany, 800 Jews were murdered in one day, and many others

Many Jews died at the hands of Christians during the Crusades. As Jews did not accept the divinity of Christ, they (like Muslims) were considered "infidels." The Crusades afforded Christians an opportunity to wipe out Jewish populations located on the path to Jerusalem.

Words to remember:

Diaspora
Mohammed
Islam
Ottoman Empire
Pope Urban II
Crusades

committed suicide. Mothers who had just given birth to babies killed their own infants immediately after delivery. Large numbers of Jews were also massacred in the cities of Mainz, Cologne, and Prague. And the killings continued once the Crusaders temporarily regained control of Jerusalem. After they had killed all the Muslims in the city, they herded all those Jews who remained into a synagogue and burned them alive.

Section Review:

1. Explain the meaning of the Diaspora.
2. What new religion swept over the Holy Land and surrounding areas after 622?
3. Why did Pope Urban II call for the First Crusade?
4. What happened to many Jewish communities that lay in the path of the Crusaders on their way to Jerusalem?

Persecution, Ghettos, and Expulsion

With the Crusades, a long period of persecution began for Jews in Europe. Out of ignorance, some Christians began to look at Jewish physical features, language, manners, diet, and rituals with a prejudicial eye. Jews were accused of kidnapping Christian children and sacrificing them to Yahweh. They were also thought to poison Christian wells, and their women were suspected of being sorceresses. They were even accused of using Christian blood as medicine and in the making of unleavened bread for the celebration of Passover.

Such widespread beliefs led to legal restrictions and even expulsion. In 1215, Pope Innocent III decreed that Jews had to dress differently to distinguish them from Christians. In some places, they were required to wear a badge of yellow cloth in the shape of a wheel or circle. In other locales, they had to wear a pointed hat known as the "Jew Hat." England in 1218 began forcing Jews to wear the distinctive yellow badge. France followed suit one year later. Soon other countries in Europe began to require Jews to wear identifying dress marks. In addition, England, France, and other countries at times completely expelled their Jewish populations.

Persecution of the Jews began in earnest during the Crusades. Many Jews were killed in *pogroms*—organized massacres of minority groups. Sometimes the flimsiest reason served to spark a pogrom. In 1243 in the German town of Belitz, the entire Jewish population was burned alive because some of them were accused of defiling a sacramental wafer. So it went throughout Germany. Violent assaults on Jews became so bad that many left and migrated to Poland and Lithuania, where pogroms had not yet begun. Some even left all they had and went back to Palestine to live under Islamic rule.

With persecution and pogroms came

ghettos. Ghettos are sections of cities where racial or minority groups are forced to live in dismal, overcrowded conditions. The Jews in many parts of Europe were forced into such ghettos, closed off by walls from other parts of the city. Ghettos remained a part of Jewish life through the Second World War.

Section Review:

1. What were several absurd accusations made against Jews during the Middle Ages?
2. What role did Pope Innocent III play in bringing humiliation to the Jews?
3. What are pogroms?
4. What are ghettos, and why were they established?

Periods of Peace and Acceptance

While it is true that the history of the Jews from ancient times on was generally one of persecution, there were periods of tolerance when they were left alone. This was especially true in Spain, which was ruled by the Moors (Muslims) for some 800 years after Mohammed founded the Islamic religion in 622. In Spain, the Jews lived in peace and prospered. Many became wealthy landowners with castles. Others rose to high positions in the government. Nearly all lived in comfort and security. Those with education and artistic talents made great contributions to Spanish life. In fact, the period from about 1000 to 1300 is referred to as the Golden Age of Spain.

After 1300, the Christians of Spain began to drive the Moors out, a task that was completed in the late 15th century. With the Moors gone, the Christians turned on the Jews. After 1492, when Spain became a unified nation under Ferdinand and Isabella, the Jews were expelled from the country.

Not until the American and French revolutions of the late 18th century did

the Jews of Europe once again enjoy a long period of peace and stability. These revolutions had spread the ideas of freedom and liberty, and many countries in Europe began to grant full

citizenship to Jews. This period of tolerance continued in most places through the 20th century. The exceptions were Poland and Russia where pogroms reached a height in the late 19th and early 20th centuries.

Section Review:

1. Which religious group ruled Spain throughout much of the Middle Ages?
2. What was life like for the Jews who lived in medieval Spain?
3. What effect did the American and French revolutions have on Jewish life in Europe?

Repression and the Zionist Movement

The revolutions that took place in America and France in the late 1700s had little effect on such countries as Poland and Russia. There, anti-Semitism, as the hatred of Jews is called, remained as entrenched as ever. So did the practice of pogroms. Thousands of innocent Jewish men, women, and children were murdered in Poland in

As the American and French revolutions of the late 18th century spread ideas of freedom and liberty, many countries in Europe began to grant full citizenship to Jews.

Words to remember:

Moors

Ferdinand and Isabella

the 19th century.

As bad as the situation was in Poland, it was worse in Russia.

Beginning in the year 1881, when Czar Alexander II was assassinated, and continuing into the early 1900s, pogroms were a frequent occurrence. During this

Theodor Herzl (above right), an Austrian Jewish lawyer and journalist, founded the Zionist Movement in 1887. Golda Meir (above left) became Prime Minister of Israel in 1969.

Words to remember:

anti-Semitism
Golda Meir
Bolsheviks
Zionist
Theodor Herzl
mandate
alfour Declaration

time, thousands of Russian Jews immigrated to the United States. One young Jewish girl, who immigrated to America in 1906, recalled huddling in fear one night on the stairwell of her home in Kiev as a crazed mob ran through the streets breaking into Jewish homes and killing the inhabitants. Her home was spared because her father, who had heard that a pogrom was in the works, had nailed boards over all the windows and doors. That young girl was Golda Meir, who in 1969 became the Prime Minister of Israel.

Other Russian Jews were not as fortunate as Golda and her family. Hundreds were killed in a pogrom that occurred in 1905. But this pales compared to the number of Jews killed during the Russian Civil War of 1918–1921. This was the civil war that brought the Bolsheviks (Communists) to power and created the Soviet Union. During that terrible period of fighting, some 2,000 pogroms occurred in which

more than 100,000 Jews were killed.

An outgrowth of the persecution and pogroms of the late 19th century was the founding of the Zionist Movement. The Zionist Movement had as its goal the formation of a Jewish nation in Palestine. It was founded in 1887 by Theodor Herzl, an Austrian Jewish lawyer and journalist. The name *Zionist* is derived from "Zion," which was a hill in ancient Jerusalem on which sat the palace of King David.

After the Zionist Movement began, thousands of Jews immigrated to Palestine. At the time, Palestine was part of the Ottoman (Turkish) Empire. Although the Turks had no plans to grant the Jews a homeland, many Jews went there anyway. In 1918, after the Turks, along with Germany and Austria-Hungary, were defeated in World War I, the British occupied Palestine. In 1922, they were given a mandate over the region. This meant that they would govern Palestine until the people who lived there were ready for self-government.

There was, however, a major snag to Palestine obtaining any degree of self-government. That was the tension between the Jews and Arabs. In 1917, Great Britain had issued what was called the Balfour Declaration. This declaration affirmed Britain's support of a Jewish homeland in Palestine. The Arabs vehemently opposed such a move, especially since the British had made them the same promise. Therefore, to appease the Arabs, the British intercepted ships carrying Jewish immigrants to Palestine and placed the passengers in camps on the island of Cyprus.

Section Review:

1. What caused thousands of Russian Jews to immigrate to the United States in the late 1800s and early 1900s?
2. Who was Golda Meir?
3. What was the goal of the Zionist Movement?

4. What was the Balfour Declaration? How did it increase tension between Jews and Arabs in Palestine?

The Holocaust

No period in the history of Jewish repression compares with the Holocaust. The word *holocaust* comes from a Greek word meaning "burnt whole" and is the term applied to the deliberate attempt of Nazi Germany to exterminate the entire Jewish population of Europe during World War II. At least 6 million Jews were murdered during this time. Some sources place the estimate as high as 8 million. (Millions of other innocent people were also murdered by the Nazis. They include Gypsies, Slavic peoples, political prisoners, and any others the Nazis decided had no right to live.)

The Holocaust resulted from the twisted ideas of Adolf Hitler. Hitler rose to power partly because of his tirades that the Jews were responsible for all of Germany's economic woes. They were also, Hitler believed, an "inferior race" that had to be eliminated for the good of all Germans. As soon as the Nazis attained power in 1933, Jews were designated "second-class citizens." They were made to wear the yellow Star of David and were barred from certain kinds of employment. Next came beatings and the burnings of Jewish homes, businesses, and synagogues. Then, concentration camps began to appear. These included such notorious names as Dachau and Buchenwald. Many Jews, along with other "undesirables," were literally worked to death in these camps.

More camps were built as the Germans overran Poland and other countries. In addition to the slow deaths in the camps, thousands of Jews were shot outright or killed in other ways. In Russia, special death squads of SS troops followed the regular German army into occupied territory and murdered more than a million Jews.

But this was only the beginning.

Although Jews in the conquered nations were being shot and killed in special gas vans, this was not quick enough to suit the Nazis. A more

"efficient" method was needed to rid Europe of its Jews. This method came into being as part of what was called the "Final Solution." It went into effect in 1942. The Final Solution called for Europe's Jews to be killed in gas chambers in special extermination camps. Although these camps were located in many places, those that murdered the most Jews were in Poland. Such names as Auschwitz, Treblinka, and Sobibor—to name three—stood as symbols of horror when they were finally liberated with the defeat of Nazi Germany during World War II. Depending on the capacity of the camp, between 12,000 and 20,000 Jews were gassed and their bodies burned every day the camps were in operation.

If the goal of the Nazis was to exterminate European Jewry, they almost succeeded. One estimate of the number of Jews in Europe at the time Hitler came to power was 9.5 million. At the most, it seems certain that less than 3 million remained alive when the Nazi terror came to an end.

Section Review:

1. What was the Holocaust?
2. How many Jews were exterminated by the Nazis during World War II?

The "Final Solution," which went into effect in 1942, called for European Jews to be killed in gas chambers in special extermination camps.

Words to remember:

Holocaust
Adolf Hitler
Final Solution

extermination camps

3. Why were the Jews singled out for persecution and death?
4. Where were the worst of the death camps located?
5. What was the Final Solution?

The State of Israel

Because of the horrors of the Holocaust, the world finally turned a sympathetic ear to the plight of the Jewish people. It is tragic that it took their almost total extermination to make people elsewhere admit that the Jews had been treated in a very bad way.

In November 1947, the United Nations decided that Palestine should be divided into a Jewish state and an Arab state. The Jews accepted this proposal, but the Arabs did not. The Arabs, not only in Palestine but throughout the Middle East, wanted the Jews out of Palestine. Therefore, within hours of Israel declaring its independence on May 15, 1948, it was attacked by the Arab states of Syria, Egypt, Lebanon, Transjordan (now Jordan), Saudi Arabia, and Iraq. After seven months of fighting, the Israelis threw back the invaders. From that time onward the nation of Israel was an established reality.

There have been three other Arab-Israeli wars since 1948. They occurred in 1956, 1967, and 1973. The Israelis emerged victors in each of them. Even though the Arab nations failed by war to dislodge the Jews from Israel, they have never stopped trying. As this book was being written, tension between the Israelis and Palestinians was at an all-time high. Suicide bombings on the part of Palestinians, followed by retaliatory strikes by the Israeli army, dominated the news.

Section Review:

1. When did Israel become an independent nation?
2. What happened when the Israelis declared their independence?
3. In your opinion, why have the Israelis prevailed over the Arabs in the wars they have fought?

For Further Thought:

1. If you had been a Christian Crusader of the 11th century, would you have done anything to stop the atrocities committed by the Crusaders against the Jews? Why or why not?
2. Imagine yourself a Jew living in a European country when the pope decreed that all Jews had to wear identifying dress. How would you have felt? Would you have been angry? Frightened? Embarrassed? Proud?
3. Pretend you are a Christian living in Europe in the 13th century. Write a letter to your local priest expressing your dismay with the decree that Jews had to dress differently than Christians.
4. Why do you think Jewish persecution was greater in eastern than in western Europe?
5. Participate in a debate. Resolved: That the German people knew about the Nazi extermination camps but did not care.
6. Why do you think much of the world turned a deaf ear to the plight of the Jews during World War II?
7. Do you think the Arabs and the Israelis will ever live side-by-side in peace? Why or why not?
8. Most observers agree that suicide bombings carried out by Arabs are acts of terrorism. Are retaliatory strikes by Israel also acts of terrorism? Why or why not?

CHAPTER FOUR

Basic Jewish Beliefs

Who is a Jew? Is a Jew a member of a religious group? Or is a Jew part of a nation in the same way that Native Americans are, sharing his or her history and language with others? No single definition seems fitting. There are those who are born Jews and those who become Jews by choice. Throughout the remainder of this book, the term "Jew" will apply to all people who adhere to Judaism as a religion. This includes those who convert to Judaism from another faith.

Although there are different branches of Judaism, all Jews share certain beliefs and truths. One is that there is one, universal God. In their services and daily prayers, Jews cite the following prayer from Deuteronomy 6:4, a prayer referred to as the Shema: "Hear O Israel, the Lord our God, the Lord is One." Jews call God Yahweh. (Some Jews use the less divine name *Adonai*, which means "Lord.") They believe Yahweh is all-knowing, without fault, and without form.

Another belief shared by all Jews is that God made a covenant with Abraham. Jews believe that God chose Abraham to be the father of a great nation in the Promised Land of Canaan. They also believe that God chose the Hebrews to receive his law, and as long as they obeyed him and followed his laws, he would look after them and protect them.

Most Jews also believe in the coming of a Messiah. Although Jesus was born a Jew and is regarded as a great teacher and storyteller, Jews do not believe he is the Messiah, or Savior. They believe the Messiah is yet to come. Orthodox Jews believe the Messiah will reward those who have accepted his leadership and obeyed the Law, and that he will punish those who have not. Certain branches of Judaism see the Messiah in a different light. These differences of opinion are discussed in Chapter Six, "Major Branches."

Other beliefs shared by Jews include the following:
- The words of the prophets are true.
- Moses was the greatest of the prophets.
- The dead will be resurrected.

Section Review:

1. What makes a person a Jew?
2. What do Jews call God?
3. What covenant do Jews believe God made with Abraham?
4. How do Jews view Jesus?

The Synagogue

The Jewish place of worship is the synagogue. *Synagogue* is derived from a Greek word meaning "assembly" or "to bring together." The synagogue also

Words to remember:

Shema
covenant
Messiah

A belief in one, universal God is central to Judaism. In their services and daily prayers, Jews recite Deuteronomy 6:4 —written below in Hebrew and English.

synagogue
Ark
Torah
Ner Tamid
menorah
bimah
rabbi
cantor

serves as a community and education center. Most synagogues have a school where Jewish children learn Hebrew and study Jewish religion, history, and literature. Many synagogues also have a library, a kitchen, and a hall for social events.

There are large synagogues and there are small synagogues. They are usually built in the architectural style of local buildings. In ancient times, synagogues were built so that a person entering for worship would be facing in the direction of Jerusalem. Today, some synagogues are built facing in that direction.

The most important part of the inside of a synagogue is the Ark. This is a wooden cabinet where the Torah scrolls are kept. (More about the Torah later.) The original ark of ancient times—the Ark of the Covenant—is said to have kept the Ten Commandments safe during the Exodus. It was an oblong box or chest made of acadia wood, and was covered inside and out in gold. It is thought to have been 3 1/2 feet long, 2 1/4 feet wide, and 2 1/4 feet high. It was carried on poles by priests when the ancient Hebrews went into battle. Any enemy who came near the Ark was supposed to have been struck dead. Where is the Ark today? No one knows for sure. According to legend, the Ark was hidden under the Temple in Jerusalem when the city fell to the Chaldeans. But there is no evidence that it was ever found when the Temple was destroyed. Later, the prophet Jeremiah was said to have hidden the Ark in a cave on the top of Mount Nebo, where it was supposed to stay until the coming of the Messiah. There is even one theory that states the Ark is hidden somewhere in Ethiopia. Many people think the Ark will never be found.

In front of the Ark hangs a lamp whose flame is never extinguished. This is the *Ner Tamid*, or the Eternal Lamp. The Ner Tamid is symbolic of the lamp that once burned in the Temple in Jerusalem. Jews believe that it reminds them that God is present. On either side of the Ark is a *menorah*, a seven-branched candlestick. The seven branches represent the number of days the Bible says it took God to create the universe. The middle branch stands for the Sabbath.

Leading up to the Ark is a raised platform called the *bimah*. It contains a table or pulpit from where services are directed. On either side are two chairs, one for the rabbi and one for the cantor. The *rabbi* is the spiritual leader of the synagogue. He (or perhaps she in Reform Judaism) conducts services on the Sabbath, holy days, and festivals. The *cantor* assists the rabbi by chanting traditional Jewish songs and prayers.

The rabbi is ordained (meaning he is declared officially to be a rabbi) by the head or faculty of the seminary he attended. He has many duties. In addition to conducting services and preachings, he helps Jews understand the Torah. He also decides questions of Jewish law, helps members of the synagogue with personal problems, and teaches Judaism to adult groups. Sometimes he is also the head of the school that is associated with the synagogue. Not the least of his duties is officiating at circumcisions, marriages, and burials.

Section Review:

1. What is the Jewish place of worship called?
2. Why was the Ark of the Covenant so important to the ancient Hebrews?
3. What happened to the Ark of the Covenant?
4. What is kept in the Ark of a modern synagogue?
5. Name any three duties performed by the rabbi.
6. What is the role of the cantor in a Jewish service?

Worshipping in a Synagogue

The Jewish Sabbath (Shabbat) begins on Friday at sundown and lasts until Saturday at sundown. This is one of the times when Jews worship in the synagogue. On the Sabbath, Jews who adhere strictly to the ancient law do not work or cook any meals. Food is prepared beforehand so it won't have to be cooked on the Sabbath. Some Jews do not watch television, use the phone, or even drive on this holiest of days. The differences in the way Jews see the Sabbath is explained in more detail in Chapter Six.

In an Orthodox Jewish synagogue, men and women sit in different sections. In a synagogue attended by Reformed Jews, men and women sit together. There is also a difference in the language of the service. The Orthodox Jewish service is conducted in Hebrew. The service of Reformed Jews is performed in the vernacular, or the common language of the people.

Clothing worn at services in the synagogue also differs. In general, however, men wear a skullcap known as a *yarmulke* or *kippa*. This is worn as a sign of respect. At morning services they also wear a prayer shawl called a *tallit*. In addition, men in Orthodox synagogues wear two small boxes with straps called *tefillin* (sometimes *tephillin*). One box is worn in the middle of the forehead to remind Jews that they must love Yahweh with all their mind. The other box is tied to the left arm facing the heart. This is to remind the worshipper that he must love Yahweh with all his heart. The boxes contain small pieces of parchment. Written on the parchment are four selections from the Old Testament. There are two selections from the book of Exodus and two from Deuteronomy. In Orthodox synagogues, women are forbidden to wear the yarmulke. They are also forbidden to wear a shawl. In other synagogues, the yarmulke and shawl are optional.

Services in a synagogue parallel in some ways worship in churches of other faiths. There are readings from the Scriptures (Old Testament) and the Torah.

There are songs and prayers. And there is a sermon presented by the rabbi.

It is an honor for members of the congregation to be asked to open the Ark and remove the Torah. The Torah contains the first five books of the Old Testament. It is written in Hebrew on strips of parchment by trained writers, taking a year to complete. The Torah is divided into 54 parts, one or two of which are read at each service. There are 792,077 letters and 410,638 crowns which decorate the letters, making for a total of

1.2 million characters in each Torah. The strips of parchment that make up the Torah cost $100 each. They are sewn together in a long scroll, which is carefully unrolled by the handles to which it is attached. No one is permitted to touch the scroll itself. Upon completion of the service, the Torah is placed back in the Ark.

The Torah found in the Ark of synagogues is called the Written Torah. Teachings contained in the Talmud, another book that interprets biblical laws

Jewish men often wear a skullcap called a *yarmulke* or *kippa*. At morning services they also wear a prayer shawl called a *tallit*. Men in Orthodox synagogues wear two small boxes with straps called *tefillin*. One box is worn in the middle of the forehead. The other is tied to the left arm facing the heart.

and commandments, is referred to as the Oral Torah. The Talmud is a collection of oral laws that were put into written form around A.D. 200.

Section Review:

1. When is the Jewish Sabbath? What is it called?
2. In what language are services in a Reformed Jewish synagogue conducted?
3. Identify, define, or explain: yarmulke; tallit; tefillin.
4. What is included in the Torah (Written Torah)?
5. How is a Torah prepared?

Obligations and Responsibilities

Jews believe that their obligations are not confined to attending services at the synagogue. Like people of other faiths, they believe they have many responsibilities to their communities. These include providing shelter for widows and orphans, helping the sick and needy, comforting the mourning, and keeping the body healthy and clean.

There are 613 *mitzvot* (commandments) listed in the Torah.

Some were written long ago and do not apply to today's world. Ten that do and which are selected at random are listed below.

- Do not profane God's name.
- Honor your father and mother.
- Honor the old and the wise.
- Circumcise male offspring.
- Do not stand idly by when a human life is in danger.
- Do not wrong anyone in speech.
- Do not cherish hatred in your heart.
- Do not take revenge.
- Do not bear a grudge.
- Do not wrong a stranger in buying and selling.

The obligations and commandments mentioned above reflect the heart of the Jewish faith. Judaism does not concern itself with a formal set of beliefs or dogma. Instead, it focuses on one's relationship to God and ethical conduct.

Section Review:

1. What are mitzvot?
2. How are the mitzvot listed at the end of this section similar to the Ten Commandments?

For Further Thought:

1. If you are not of the Jewish faith, how is worship in a synagogue different from that in your place of worship? How is it similar? Write a brief report pointing out such differences and similarities.
2. Research "Torah Scribes," or writers, on either the Internet or in a book on Judaism. Write a report on their work in producing Torahs.
3. One of the mitzvot or commandments in the Torah instructs Jews not to seek revenge. In your opinion, have the Israelis betrayed or violated that commandment by retaliating against Arab invaders and terrorists throughout their brief history? Why or why not?
4. Do you think Orthodox Jews discriminate against women by requiring them to sit in a separate section in the synagogue? Why or why not?
5. Discuss other religious faiths or churches that disapprove of work on the Sabbath. Do you know of people who adhere to this restriction?
6. Research and write a report on the Ark of the Covenant.
7. Many Christians blame the Jews for the death of Christ? Is this a fair accusation? Why or why not?

CHAPTER FIVE

Family Life and Customs

Since ancient times, the family has been the center of Jewish life. In early Hebrew history, however, home life comprised the extended family. This meant that grandparents, parents, and their sons, wives, and children all lived under the same roof. As time passed, however, the importance of the extended family waned. This has been especially true in places such as the United States, where the children of Jewish parents tend to move from the family home.

But despite the decline of the extended family, as well as the differences between the various branches of Judaism, all Jews share certain rituals and ceremonies. These ceremonies begin at birth and continue to death. In this chapter, you will learn about these and other aspects of Jewish life.

Inside the Home

Jews are no different from Christians and others in the way they follow their religion's teachings inside the home. In many Christian homes, for example, grace is said before each meal. In some Christian homes, this is not done. The same applies to prayer and the reading of the Bible. Many Christians pray and read their Bible everyday. Others do not. In addition, many Christians faithfully attend church every Sunday. Others seldom do. So it is with Jewish families. Many follow the strict teachings of the ancient Hebrews, while others do not. This chapter attempts to address Jewish homes in general.

As you approach the door of a Jewish home, you might see a decorative, oblong box made of wood, metal, or glass that is fastened to the right-hand side of the doorjamb. Inside the box is a tiny

parchment scroll called a *mezuzah*. On this tiny scroll is inscribed the Shema prayer (see Chapter Four, paragraph two). You will also find mezuzahs attached to the doors of every room except the bathroom. Traditional Jews feel that by touching the mezuzah they are reminded of God's presence.

Of utmost importance to most Jews is the celebration of the Shabbat. They believe that the importance and holiness

Jewish homes sometimes have a decorative, oblong box made of wood, metal, or glass fastened to the right-hand side of the doorjamb. Inside the box is a tiny scroll called a *mezuzah* on which is inscribed a prayer.

mezuzah
challah
kiddush
havdalah
kosher

Foods that Jews are
allowed to eat are listed
in the book of Leviticus
in the Old Testament.

of the day is emphasized in the fourth commandment, which reads "Remember the Sabbath Day to keep it holy. Six days shall you labor and do all thy work, but the seventh day is a Sabbath Day unto the Lord thy God" (Exodus 20:8–11).

Especially important is the special Shabbat meal that is eaten on Friday evening. All cooking for the meal is done on Thursday. Then on Friday, the house is cleaned and the table is set. The table is covered with a white cloth, on which are placed the best dishes and silverware in the house. Two candles and a cup of wine are also set out, and there are two loaves of specially baked braided bread called *challah*. There are also other specially prepared foods that are eaten. Before the meal begins, the head of the household says the kiddush prayer. The purpose of this prayer is to give thanks for the Shabbat and the challah. The

family celebration of the Shabbat ends on Saturday evening when the head of the house recites a prayer called the *havdalah*. A special candle is lit, and there is a spice box that spreads its aroma throughout the house. The Shabbat ends when the candle is extinguished by dipping it into a cup of wine.

All foods eaten by Jews, whether during the Shabbat or at other times, must be kosher. *Kosher* means "fitting" or "proper." Foods that Jews are allowed to eat are listed in the book of Leviticus in the Old Testament. Kosher foods include all fruits and vegetables, fish with both scales and fins, and the meat of animals that chew their cud and have cleft hooves, such as cows and sheep. Animals that do not fall into this category, such as pigs and rabbits, may not be eaten. Shellfish are also on the forbidden list.

Animals that are eaten must be killed swiftly and in a humane way. Then their

meat must be soaked and salted to remove all the blood. At no time may meat and dairy products be eaten at the same meal. Some kitchens even have separate sinks so that these foods are never mixed. In addition, separate utensils are used in their preparation and serving.

What is the basis for these dietary laws? Some scholars believe they began for health reasons. Others think that the killing of animals as quickly and as humanely as possible taught sympathy for all living things. Still others feel that strict laws were put in effect to keep the ancient Hebrews from eating the same foods as pagans. Whatever the reasons, the laws have been one of the factors that have helped Jews maintain their separate identity through the ages.

Section Review:

1. What is the significance of a mezuzah?
2. What is challah?
3. When is the kiddush prayer recited? The havdalah?
4. What are kosher foods?
5. What kinds of meat are Jews forbidden to eat?

Special Ceremonies

From birth to the ages of 12 and 13, Jewish girls and boys pass through several important stages in their young lives. These stages consist of rituals that initiate them into the Jewish way of life.

On the Sabbath following a baby girl's birth, she is taken to the synagogue, where she is given a name. In a Reform Jewish synagogue, a more formal ceremony has developed called *Berit Hahayyim*, or "covenant of life." As the infant girl is brought into the synagogue, those in attendance greet her by saying "Blessed is she who comes." This is similar to the welcome infant boys receive when the audience announces "Blessed be he who comes."

Introduction to life is a little more

involved for a Jewish baby boy. When he is eight days old, he undergoes the ritual of circumcision. Circumcision is a relatively minor operation in which the foreskin at the end of the penis is removed. Often this is

done in the synagogue, either by a doctor or a trained rabbi. If the baby boy is ill on the eighth day of his life, the circumcision is put off until he is well. At the time of circumcision, the baby boy is given a name. The ritual of circumcision is referred to as *Brit* (or *Berit*) *Milah*. It is performed because Jews believe it stems from a covenant Abraham made with God. (See Genesis 17:9–13.) After the procedure, a festive meal is eaten.

The next important ritual in the life of a Jewish child occurs when a girl is 12 and a boy is 13. This ritual is called Bat Mitzvah for a girl and Bar Mitzvah for a boy. It is a "coming of age" ritual that signifies the passage from childhood to

Occurring when a girl is 12 and a boy is 13, Bat Mitzvah (for a girl) and Bar Mitzvah (for a boy) signifies the passage to adulthood.

Words to remember:

Berit Hahayyim
Brit Milah
Bat Mitzvah
Bar Mitzvah
Confirmation

adulthood. *Bat Mitzvah* means "daughter of the commandment," while *Bar Mitzvah* means "son of the commandment." *Bar* is the word for "boy" and *bat* (or *bas*) for "girl." *Mitzvah* means "commandment."

The ceremony of Bat Mitzvah for girls was not initiated until the 1940s, but Bar Mitzvah has been a part of a young boy's religious maturity since the fifth or sixth century. Months before the ritual, a Jewish boy prepares himself by studying Hebrew. On the first Sabbath following his 13th birthday, he takes an active part in the religious service. He may read passages from the Torah and the prophets. He may also lead a prayer or perform some other part of the service.

Jewish weddings often take place under a canopy called a huppah.

Generally, he gives a speech, which he begins with the phrase "today I am a man." Bar Mitzvah is an important and happy occasion. After the ceremony,

there is a reception, and the newly recognized adult receives gifts from his parents and friends.

Conservative and Reform Jews have Bat Mitzvah for girls. In a Conservative Jewish synagogue, the ritual for a girl is similar to that for a boy, except that the girl does not read from the Torah. In a Reform Jewish synagogue, there is no distinction between Bar Mitzvah and Bat Mitzvah. Girls are accorded the same honor as boys.

Most Conservative, all Reform Jews, and some Orthodox Jews, also have a Confirmation ceremony. This is a rite for both boys and girls when they reach the age of 16. Confirmation is a time when young people publicly announce their dedication to Judaism.

Section Review:

1. What is the basis for the Brit Milah ceremony?
2. What do Bar Mitzvah and Bat Mitzvah signify? At what age do they occur?
3. How do Reform Jews differ from others in their practice of Bar Mitzvah and Bat Mitzvah?
4. What is the reason for the Confirmation ceremony?

Marriage

Jews believe that marriage is a sacred relationship demanded by God. They believe that Yahweh early on commanded the Hebrews to marry and have children to increase the number of people who worshiped him. They base this belief on Genesis 1:27–28, which reads in part:

Be fruitful, and multiply, and replenish the earth.

Some Jewish marriage ceremonies are more traditional and formal than others. In general, however, the marriage takes place under a canopy called a *huppah*. The wedding may be held either in the synagogue, in the home, or out of doors. A cup of wine is drunk as the rabbi recites the betrothal blessing. The blessing concludes with the sentence "Blessed are you, O Lord our God, who sanctifies his people Israel by means of the wedding canopy and the sacred rites of marriage."

After the bride and groom share the cup of wine, the groom places a ring on the bride's left hand. As he does so, he says: "Behold, you are consecrated to me by this ring as my wife according to the law of Moses and Israel." If there is a *ketubah*, or marriage contract, this is then read by the rabbi. Finally, the rabbi recites the *sheva berakhot*, or wedding blessings. This is done over a second glass of wine. The wedding ends with the groom stomping on and breaking the wineglass. The reason for this symbolic act is two-fold. First, it is to remind the couple that, despite their happiness, they are not to forget the sufferings of the Jewish people throughout history. And second, it is a reminder that the First and Second Temples in Jerusalem were destroyed in ancient times. With the breaking of the glass, the guests shout "mazel tov!" (Congratulations!)

Weddings in Conservative and Reform Jewish communities are somewhat different from the more Orthodox Jewish wedding. Many Conservative and Reform Jewish weddings are double-ring ceremonies in which the bride also places a ring on the groom's finger. When she does, she recites words similar to those of the groom: "Behold, you are consecrated to me by this ring as my husband according to the law of Moses and Israel."

Section Review:

1. How did Jews come to believe that marriage is ordained by God?
2. What is the name for the canopy under which a Jewish wedding takes place?
3. What is a ketubah?

4. What is the significance of a Jewish groom stepping on and breaking a wineglass at the conclusion of the wedding ceremony?
5. How are some Conservative and Reform Jewish weddings different from those of Orthodox Jews?

A Jewish wedding ends with the groom stomping on a wineglass as the guests shout "mazel tov!"

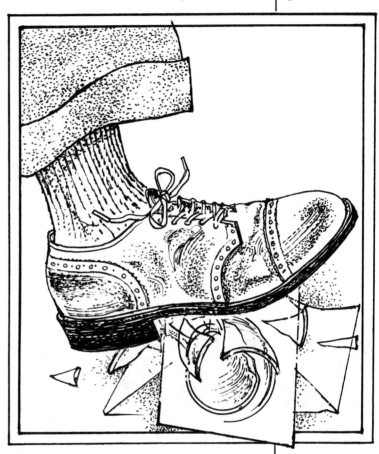

Customs at Death

Jewish burials are simple affairs. Since, as Jews point out, death comes to everyone and is therefore a great equalizer, little distinction is made between the rich and the poor.

Funerals are scheduled as soon as possible. This often takes place within 24 hours. The deceased is dressed in a simple white garment and buried in a plain coffin. There are no flowers. In traditional funerals, the procession accompanying the coffin to the grave stops seven times, while Psalm 91 is recited. (Part of this Psalm is a promise that those who have led good lives and obeyed the laws of God will go to Heaven.) The burial service itself consists of prayers, a eulogy, and the Kaddish, which is a prayer of mourning. Following the funeral, the family of the deceased retires for a week of deep mourning. This week is referred to as *shiva*. Orthodox Jews sit on special low stools; men do not shave and women do not use makeup. Relatives and friends bring food to the house and conduct services. Even after shiva, the family continues to mourn. Those who work return to their labors after the thirteenth day, but they do not attend social gatherings for a while. Sometimes a son or daughter will continue to mourn the death of a parent for a year. One year after the funeral, mourners assemble in the synagogue for a special memorial service. Also at this time, a simple tombstone is put at the grave of the deceased.

Although Jews believe in life after death, they place more emphasis on life on earth. They think it is of more importance to concentrate on doing good while they are living than to concern themselves with what happens after death.

Orthodox Jews observe shiva—a week of deep mourning—following the death of a loved one. During shiva, Jews retreat from the normal routines of life and do not work or socialize. They sit on special low stools; men do not shave and women do not wear makeup. Relatives and friends bring food to the house and conduct services.

Section Review:

1. How soon after death are Jewish funerals held?
2. What is the Kaddish?
3. What takes place during shiva?
4. How long does a son or daughter mourn the loss of a parent?

For Further Thought:

1. Compare Jewish observance of the Sabbath with that of other faiths. If your family is religious, how do they celebrate the Sabbath?
2. Throughout history, the ages 12/13 have usually signified a child's passage into adulthood. Why do you think this is so?
3. Do you think Orthodox Jews discriminate against girls by not having a Bat Mitzvah? Why or why not?
4. Should all engaged couples—Jewish or otherwise—be required to sign a marriage contract specifying the rights and duties of each? Write a report giving your views on the subject.
5. Should all weddings be two-ringed ceremonies? Why or why not? Why might this be important to some people?
6. How do the views and rituals concerning death as practiced by the Jews and other faiths compare to those of ancient societies?

CHAPTER SIX

Major Branches

There have always been different branches or sects of Judaism. In ancient times, there were the Pharisees and Sadducees. Then, in the 18th century, other branches, such as Hasidism, began to spring up. Hasidic Judaism developed in the Ukraine in Russia during the time of terrible pogroms against the Jews. Because Jewish rabbis and intellectuals tended to look down upon the downtrodden Russian poor, a branch of Judaism was born that placed prayer and faith on an equal level with knowledge of the law.

And so it has gone. Modern times and technology have resulted in different interpretations of the Torah and the Talmud. This has led to the emergence of distinct branches of Judaism. In the United States, these branches may be categorized as Orthodox, Reform, and Conservative.

Orthodox Judaism

In Chapter Four, you were introduced to some of the practices of Orthodox Jews. You learned, for example, that in an Orthodox synagogue, men and women sit separately. The men sit downstairs, while the women often sit in an upstairs gallery. You also learned that men wear a skullcap called a yarmulke and a prayer shawl called a tallit. In Chapter Five, you read about the way Orthodox Jews view such matters as Bar Mitzvahs, marriage, death, and mourning. Now, in Chapter Six, you will gain a better understanding of the basic principles of Orthodox Judaism.

In religious terms, the word *Orthodox* means "adhering to traditional beliefs and customs." And that is the core of Orthodox Judaism. The term was first

A man in Orthodox Jewish dress.

used in the early 19th century after Reform and Conservative Judaism developed. Since the 16th century, Orthodox Jews have followed the laws, customs, and ceremonies set forth in the *Shulhan Arukh*. The Shulhan Arukh is a kind of handbook for Jews. It was drawn up by Joseph Karo, a Talmudic scholar who lived from 1488 to 1575. It became the core of Jewish law, addressing such matters as prayer, holidays, customs, marriage, dietary laws, and other concerns.

Basically, the center of Orthodoxy states that Jews were chosen over all other nations by God to receive his law. Because they believe they are the chosen people, they have specific rules to follow and obligations to fulfill. Not the least of these is the weekly observance of the Sabbath. To the Orthodox Jew, this is a

Words to remember:

Shulhan Arukh
Joseph Karo
kashrut
treyf

most sacred time—a time when no work is done, no meals are prepared, and no other activities are engaged in. If you remember from Chapter Four, some Orthodox Jews even refrain from watching television, using the phone, or driving a car on the Sabbath.

Orthodox Jews follow the *kashrut*, the strict dietary code that began in ancient times. You have already learned that some foods are *kosher* or "clean." Foods not considered kosher are said to be *treyf*, or "unclean." Distinctions between kosher and treyf are made with regard to all forms of meat. Cow, duck, goose, pheasant, chicken, turkey, bass, cod, and tuna are kosher. Pig, eel, lobster, oyster, catfish, clams, shark, squid, shrimp, and scallops are not. As you also learned in Chapter Four, meat and milk are kept separate and never eaten at the same meal.

Words to remember:

Abraham Geiger
Israel Jacobson

Isaac
Meyer Wise

Messianic Era
minyan

Reform Jews believe that Judaism must change to fit the times. This includes granting women full rights, including the right to be ordained as rabbis.

Section Review:

1. When was the term "Orthodox Judaism" first used?
2. Who was Joseph Karo?
3. What is the kashrut?
4. What kinds of food are considered to be treyf?

Reform Judaism

Reform Judaism began in the late 18th century as a direct result of the American and French Revolutions. With ideas of political and social freedom spreading throughout Europe, it was only natural that religious thought would also be affected.

A new way of looking at the beliefs of Judaism first surfaced in what is now Germany. It grew out of the desire on the part of some Jewish scholars and rabbis to bring Judaism in line with modern times. Chief among these scholars were Israel Jacobson (1768-1828) and Abraham Geiger (1810-1874). Jacobson was the first to introduce such changes in his synagogue with the use of an organ and a mixed choir. He also recited some prayers and delivered his sermon in German. A few years later, Geiger did the same in his synagogue in Wiesbaden, Germany. In 1846, the Reform Movement was brought to America by Isaac Mayer Wise, a rabbi from Bohemia. (Bohemia became a part of Czechoslovakia when that nation was carved out of the Austro-Hungarian Empire after World War I.)

What do Reform Jews believe? Because many feel that the acceptance of any particular belief or practice is up to the individual, it is difficult to agree on a precise set of beliefs. But there are certain principles that all Reform Jews seem to agree on. Some have already been mentioned in Chapter Four. The most important of these are:

● Jewish law is not binding.
● Judaism must change to fit the times.
● Women should have full rights, including the right to become rabbis.

- Services should be conducted in the vernacular—the language of the people.
- Men and women should sit together in the synagogue, and men should not be distinguished by the wearing of yarmulkes and tallits.
- Instead of a personal Messiah, there will be a Messianic Era when equality, freedom, and brotherhood will characterize a perfect world achieved by scientific and cultural progress.
- Unlike Orthodox Judaism, a minyan (ten men) is not necessary for worship in the synagogue.

Conservative Judaism was an attempt to bridge the gap between Orthodox and Reform Judaism. Rabbi Frankel and others felt that Orthodox Judaism was too strict in its adherence

to ancient Jewish law. At the same time, he saw Reform Judaism as too liberal. He did not agree with the Reformists' view that ancient Jewish laws were not binding. He felt that such laws were indeed binding but that they could be changed somewhat to meet the needs of modern society. The way Conservative and Reform Jews look at the law is the basic difference between the two groups.

Conservative Judaism first appeared in Germany when Zechariah Frankel (1801–1875) founded the Historical School of Jewish Learning in 1850.

Section Review:

1. Where did Reform Judaism begin?
2. What connection was there between 18th-century revolutions and the beginning of Reform Judaism?
3. What is meant by the "Messianic era"?

Conservative Judaism

Like Reform Judaism, Conservative Judaism first appeared in Germany. It began when Zechariah Frankel (1801–1875) founded the Historical School of Jewish Learning in 1850. It was transported to America in the years before World War I.

Section Review:

1. Who founded Conservative Judaism?
2. What is the major difference between Conservative and Reform Judaism?

Words to remember:

Zechariah Franke

For Further Thought:

1. If you were converting to Judaism, which branch would you lean to: Orthodox, Reform, or Conservative? Why? If you already belong to one of the branches of Judaism and were going to change to another, to which branch would you change? Why?
2. Tell why you agree or disagree with religious services—Jewish or otherwise—being conducted in the vernacular, the everyday language of the people.
3. Research and explain how Jewish dietary laws are similar to those of Muslims.
4. Does your religion or denomination have any dietary restrictions, either on a permanent basis or on special days or occasions? If so, how many people do you think strictly follow them?

CHAPTER SEVEN

Holy Days

Not counting the Sabbath, the Jewish calendar lists 13 holy days and festivals. The most important of these are Rosh Hashanah, Yom Kippur, Sukkot, Hanukkah, Purim, and Pesach, or Passover. These are explained in some detail in this chapter, while others are mentioned briefly.

The High Holy Days

Jews refer to two holidays as the "High Holy Days." These are Rosh Hashanah and Yom Kippur. Rosh Hashanah is the Jewish New Year. Yom Kippur is the Day of Atonement. The latter is a day when Jews reflect on what they have done wrong during the year and ask God for forgiveness. Rosh Hashanah and Yom Kippur begin and end what are known as the Ten Days of Penitence.

The blowing of the ram's horn or shofar reminds Jews of the power of God and marks the beginning of Rosh Hashanah.

Rosh Hashanah

Rosh Hashanah occurs in either late September or early October. It is celebrated on the first and second days of the Jewish month of Tishri. (More is said about the Jewish calendar in the "For Further Thought" section at the end of the chapter.) It is a Day of Judgement, when the fate of each Jew is determined. Penitence and prayer, however, can change the verdict before Yom Kippur rolls around nine days later.

The two days of Rosh Hashanah (Reform and Conservative Jews celebrate only one day) are known by various names. Some call them the "Days of Awe." Others use the expression "Days of Judgment." Still others refer to the time as "The Day of the Sounding of the Shofar." The shofar is a hollowed ram's horn that is blown at the beginning of the special synagogue service that marks the holiday. The sounding of the shofar reminds Jews of the power of God. It also reminds them that it is time to repent of their sins.

Jews have a special meal at home on the eve of Rosh Hashanah. Part of the meal consists of apples dipped in honey. This is done to wish each member of the family a sweet and pleasant year. Also on the eve of the holiday, Jews greet each other with "may you be inscribed with a good year." Some Jews even send each other Rosh Hashanah greeting cards.

On the afternoon of the first day of Rosh Hashanah, Jews assemble at a river or other body of water for the Tashlikh (casting off) ceremony. This is a ceremony in which according to tradition, Jews symbolically cast or throw their sins into the water.

Yom Kippur

Yom Kippur takes place on Tishri 10, nine days after Rosh Hashanah. It is referred to as the "Day of Atonement." It is the holiest day in the Jewish year, a day when Jews pray all day and fast. It is the only day in the year when Jews kneel to pray.

Yom Kippur is known as Shabbat Shabbaton, the "sabbath of sabbaths." It is a day of complete rest. Jews who follow its restrictions completely do not work, cook, bathe, or engage in any pleasurable activity. They also fast from sundown of the ninth day of Tishri to sunset of the tenth day. During this time, they think of their sins, repent, and ask for forgiveness.

There is a special service in the synagogue to celebrate Yom Kippur. The ark and reading desk are covered in white cloths, and the rabbi and cantor are dressed in white. At the conclusion of the service, the shofar is blown to remind people of their promises to lead a good life throughout the coming year.

Section Review:

1. Why are Rosh Hashanah and Yom Kippur considered the holiest of Jewish holidays?
2. During which Jewish month do Rosh Hashanah and Yom Kippur take place?
3. What is a shofar?
4. Why do Jews eat apples dipped in honey on the eve of Rosh Hashanah?
5. What takes place at the Tashlikh ceremony?
6. Why do Jews celebrate Yom Kippur?

Hanukkah

Hanukkah is not the next holiday in the Jewish calendar, but to people who are non-Jewish, it is one of the best known. It begins on the 25th day of the month of Kislev and continues for eight days until the third of Trivet. This time corresponds roughly to December 12-19

in the Gregorian, or western, calendar. Hanukkah is also spelled "Hannuka" or "Chanukah." The word itself means "dedication," and it refers to the Jews rededicating the Temple in Jerusalem after their defeat of the Syrians in 165 B.C.

You will recall from Chapter One that the history of the early Jews in Jerusalem was one of being controlled by one empire after another. The Chaldeans

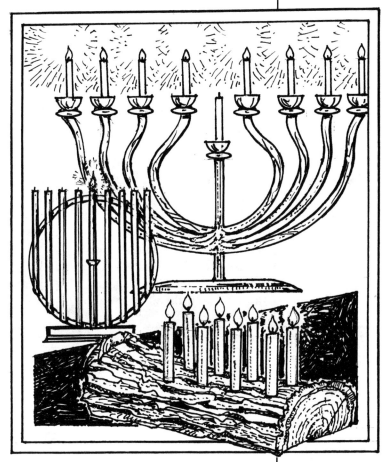

conquered the city in the 6th century B.C., to be followed by the Persians and then the Macedonian Greeks under Alexander the Great. The Greeks ruled Judea (Judah) and Jerusalem from 333 B.C. until a Jewish revolt in 165 B.C. resulted in a brief period of independence. (The Romans took control of the area in the 1st century B.C.)

It was this revolt that began in 167 B.C. that formed the basis for the celebration of Hanukkah. The revolt came about because the Syrian Greeks had

Words to remember:

Rosh Hashanah
Tishri
shofar
Yom Kippur
Tashlikh

The central ritual of Hanukkah—sometimes called the "Festival of Lights"—is the lighting of the menorah. Hanukkah means "dedication" and refers to the rededicating of the temple in Jerusalem after the Jews defeated the Syrians in 165 B.C.

tried to force the Jews to worship Greek gods. Not only did the Syrian king, Antiochus Epiphanes, not permit the Jews to follow their own religion, he ordered that pigs be sacrificed at the altar in the Temple. Because Jews consider the pig an unclean animal, they felt that the Temple had been defiled in the worst way. Led by a man named Judah, they revolted. They fought Antiochus's powerful armies for three years, winning out in the end. They were called "Maccabees" because *maccabee* is the Jewish name for "hammer," which was Judah's nickname.

When the Jews regained control of the Temple in Jerusalem in 165 B.C., they cleaned it carefully and prepared it for worship. Then they discovered that there was only enough oil to burn the lamp for one day. A party was sent out to try to find more oil. When they returned after eight days, they found, to their surprise, that the lamp was still burning. A lamp that should have burned out in one day had burned for eight. The Jews considered this a miracle. They believed that God had made the lamp burn for so long on so little oil to show his

satisfaction with them for making the Temple ready for worship again.

So that is how Hanukkah began. It celebrates both the victory over the Syrian Greeks and the rededication of the Temple. Each night of the eight-day holiday, Jews light a candle on a special nine-branched menorah called a *Hanukkiah*. (The branch in the middle holds the candle that is used to light the others.) On the first night, one candle is lit. On the second night, two candles are lit. Before the lighting of each candle, special prayers are said. And so it goes until the eighth night, when all the candles are lit and burning. Because of the candle-lighting ceremony, Hanukkah is often called the Feast or Festival of Lights.

Hanukkah is a happy festival, especially for children. There are parties and people eat foods fried in oil, such as doughnuts and potato pancakes. Many Jews also exchange gifts and make contributions to the poor.

Section Review:

1. Why do Jews celebrate Hanukkah?
2. Why did the ancient Jews revolt against the Syrian king?
3. What is the origin of the word *Maccabee*?
4. Why is *Hanukkah* called the "Festival of Lights"?

Sukkot and Simchat Torah

Sukkot is the Feast of the Tabernacles. It is celebrated five days after Yom Kippur and continues for one week. Simchat (or Simhat) Torah, or the Rejoicing of the Torah, takes place the day after Sukkot ends.

Sukkot

Sukkot was originally celebrated in ancient times at the end of the harvest season. As a show of thanksgiving, the Hebrews took offerings of fruit to the

Words to remember:

Hanukkah
Kislev
Trivet

Alexander the Great

Antiochus Epiphanes

Maccabees

Hanukkiah

To celebrate Sukkot, some Jews build huts as a reminder of how the Hebrews lived during their years as wanderers in the wilderness.

Temple. Today, fruit is still a major part of this holiday.

Sukkot begins on the 15th day of Tishri and lasts for nine days. In Israel and among Reform Jews, however, it is celebrated for only eight days. During this time, some Jews build huts or tabernacles (temporary shelters) in their gardens. They construct these huts as a reminder of how the Hebrews lived in tabernacles while they wandered in the wilderness after the Exodus from Israel. The Jewish word for "hut" or "tabernacle" is *sukkah*, the plural of which is *sukkot*. Hence the name for the festival.

The sukkah has a roof made of leaves and branches. From the roof is hung fruit, and perhaps paper chains and candy. It is built in such a way as to permit the stars to shine through. Jews live or eat in the sukkah for a week.

When Jews assemble at the synagogue to celebrate Sukkot, they have with them lulavs and etrogs. Lulavs are palm branches with sprigs of willow and myrtle. Etrogs are citrons, fruits similar to lemons. During the service, people walk around the synagogue carrying the lulav in their right hand and the etrog in their left. All four of the objects—palm, willow, myrtle, and citron—serve as symbols that God expects them to worship him with every part of their body.

The eighth day of Sukkot is called *Shemini Atzeret*. In ancient times, it was a day of thanksgiving prayer for the rain that made the crops grow.

Simchat Torah

Simchat Torah is celebrated on the ninth day of Sukkot (the eighth day in Israel and among Reform Jews). It is not a separate holiday, but because of its importance, we are treating it as such. It falls on the 23rd day of the month of Tishri.

Simchat Torah is a holy day that marks the end of the annual cycle of the readings from the Torah. After the last passage of the Pentateuch is read, the

Torah is rolled back to its beginning for the next Sabbath, when the readings begin all over again. All the

scrolls are taken out of the Ark and carried around the synagogue by the people. Children especially enjoy Simchat Torah, for they are given bags of candy and fruit.

Section Review:

1. Why do Jews build huts in their gardens when they celebrate Sukkot?
2. Describe the roof of a sukkah.
3. What is a lulav? An etrog?
4. What is the significance of the Simchat Torah festival?

Purim and Pesach

Purim is the "Feast of Lots." It falls on the fourteenth day of the month of Adar. Its name comes from the Persian word *pur* which means "lot." The name came about because of a plot to kill all the Jews in Persia many years ago. *Pesach* is another name for "Passover." It commemorates the Jews' escape from

During Simchat Torah, the Torah is taken from the Ark and carried around the synagogue.

Words to remember:

Sukkot
sukkah
lulavs
etrogs
Shemini Atzeret
Simchat Torah

slavery in Egypt. It is celebrated from the 15th to the 22nd day of the month of Nisan. In the Gregorian calendar, this corresponds to sometime in March or April, or about the same time as Easter.

The Angel of Death is said to have passed over the houses of Hebrews who had heeded Moses' plea to smear their thresholds with lamb's blood.

Purim

The story about how the festival of Purim began comes from the Book of Esther in the Old Testament. It concerns Haman, the chief minister to King Ahasuerus of Persia. (In history books, Ahasuerus is known by the Greek name Xerxes.) Haman did not like the Jews and wanted to have all of them killed. He told King Ahasuerus that the Jews in Persia showed no respect for their rulers and were even plotting against them. Ahasuerus believed him and told him to set a date for their executions. Because Haman had a difficult time making up his mind, he decided to select the day by lot. (To choose by lot means to write

numbers or names on pieces of paper or other objects, place them in a container, and pick one.) The day chosen was the 14th day of the 12th month, which was the month of Adar.

Haman had runners sent to all parts of the Persian Empire with orders to put all Jews to the sword on the appointed day. But because of the intervention of Queen Esther, Ahasuerus's wife, the executions never came about. Her husband did not know it, but Esther was a Jew, and she was determined to save her people. She went to Ahasuerus and told him of Haman's trickery. Ahasuerus believed her, and although Haman's orders had already gone out, he allowed the Jews to obtain weapons to defend themselves. The Jews fought bravely and triumphantly, killing some 75,000 of the king's soldiers in the process. Haman was put to death for his scheming.

The festival of Purim is a two-day event. On the 14th day of Adar, Jews fast. But the 15th day is a day of prayer and merrymaking. At the synagogue, the story of how the Jews of Persia were saved is read from the Book of Esther. At each mention of Haman's name, people boo and stamp their feet, and children twirl noisemakers called greggors (or gragers). The idea is to make so much noise that Haman's name cannot be heard.

Children often attend parties on Purim. Sometimes they also put on plays that relate the story of how the Jews were saved. One custom associated with the festival is mishloach manot, a practice in which gifts of food and money are sent to the poor.

Pesach

Pesach (Passover) has been celebrated by Jews since the Exodus from Egypt. The word *Passover* comes from Moses telling the Hebrews in Egypt to smear the doorjambs of their houses with lamb's blood. That way, the Angel of Death would "pass over" the house and spare the first-born child. (See Chapter

One for a review of the tenth plague visited upon the Egyptians—the plague that called for the death of every first-born child.)

Before Passover begins, Jews clean their houses and remove all leavened bread. Even small crumbs are swept up with a feather and burned. During the week of the festival, they eat only matzah, or unleavened bread. This is in remembrance of the flight from Egypt, when Jews left in such a hurry they did not have time to add yeast to the dough to make it rise.

The most important part of Pesach is the Seder meal. This is a meal that includes foods that Jews eat at no other time of the year. Each food serves as a symbol of the period of slavery in Egypt. As the meal is eaten, the story of the Passover and the Exodus from Egypt is read from the Haggadah. The Haggadah is a special book that is only read during Pesach. The youngest child in the family has the honor of asking four questions, which are answered during the reading. These questions and answers relate the story of Passover. At the conclusion of the meal, the family stays at the table and sings special songs.

Section Review:

1. Why is *Purim* called the "Feast of Lots"?
2. What role do "greggors" play in the celebration of Purim?
3. What is the origin of *Passover*?
4. Why do Jews eat only unleavened bread during Pesach?
5. What story is told during the eating of the seder meal?

Other Jewish holidays include Shavout, which celebrates the giving of the Ten Commandments to Moses on Mount Sinai; Tu B'Shevat, which is the Jewish Arbor Day, and Tisha B'Av, a day of fasting and mourning as a reminder of the destruction of the first and second Temples.

Words to remember:

Purim
Adar
Nisan
King Ahasuerus
Haman
Esther
greggors
mishloach manot
matzah
Pesach
Seder
Haggadah

For Further Thought:

1. How does a lunar calendar—the kind used by Jews—differ from the Gregorian, or western calendar, that is used throughout most of the world?
2. Make a chart comparing the months of the Jewish calendar with those of the Gregorian calendar. Consult either an encyclopedia, the Internet, or a book on Judaism for information.
3. Compare/contrast the Jewish New Year with the New Year observed by Christians and other religious groups.
4. Research the Seder meal, the meal eaten by Jews on the first night of Pesach. Write a brief report about the foods eaten and the significance of each.
5. Judaism, like many religions, places great emphasis on helping the poor and needy. Do you think help for the less fortunate should come from religious and/or charitable groups, or do you think this should be a function of government? Give reasons why you think as you do.
6. Suppose newspapers existed at the time the ancient Jews defeated the Syrians and reclaimed the Temple in Jerusalem. Also suppose that you are a reporter for the *Jerusalem Star*. In accordance with Jewish belief that the lamp in the Temple burned for eight days when there was only enough oil for one day, write an article based on an interview you had with someone who witnessed the event.
7. If you were a very young child, which Jewish holiday would you look forward to the most? Why?

CHAPTER EIGHT

Jewish Contributions

Any study of Jewish contributions to history is probably best divided into two long periods: the 4000-plus years of ancient times and the almost-2000 years since. Jewish achievements in ancient times were mainly in the fields of religion and religious writings. Since that time, however, Jews have made outstanding contributions in music, art, literature, science, entertainment, sports, and other fields. This chapter summarizes some of the most significant Jewish contributions.

The Early Hebrews

Unlike other ancient civilizations, the early Hebrews made no great achievements in such fields as science, architecture, or engineering. But what they contributed to religion and religious literature far overshadows any

The Ten Commandments have shaped the laws of almost every society in the world.

contributions they might have made in other areas.

Perhaps the greatest contribution of the early Hebrews was the idea of *monotheism*. Monotheism is the belief in one god. As you have probably learned in your history classes, ancient peoples worshiped a pantheon of gods. This means they had a whole family of deities they bowed down to. There were gods of the sun, the moon, the sky, the ocean, and the harvest, to name a few. There was a god (or a goddess) for just about everything. The belief in and worship of many gods is called *polytheism*.

The kind of monotheism formed by the early Hebrews is sometimes called *ethical monotheism*. This is because it placed emphasis on ethics, or proper conduct. The Hebrews believed that Yahweh, or God, was a just and loving god who cared for his people, but, who, at the same time, demanded righteous behavior. This behavior was outlined in the Ten Commandments, which Jews believe Moses received from God at the top of Mount Sinai. The Ten Commandments, along with a group of laws developed during the period of Judges (the time before the Hebrews had a king), came to make up Mosaic Law, or the Law of Moses. Mosaic Law is another great contribution of the ancient Hebrews. The Ten Commandments, of which it is a part, have shaped the laws of almost every society throughout history.

A final contribution of the early Hebrews is the Old Testament. It is made up of 39 books that relate the history of the Jewish people. Jews divide the Old Testament into three parts. These parts are the Torah, the Prophets, and the Writings. You learned in Chapter Four that the first five books of the Old Testament are called the Pentateuch. These are the books that are included in the Torah. The Old Testament has had a great impact on western civilization, and many of its ideas helped form the foundation of Christianity.

Section Review:

1. How are monotheism and polytheism different?
2. Of what is Mosaic Law comprised?
3. Into what 3 parts do Jews divide the Old Testament?

Contemporary Contributions

Jews living in both the state of Israel and the Diaspora in modern times have made outstanding contributions to humankind. Many have been awarded Nobel Prizes. They include Albert Einstein and Enrico Fermi in physics and Selman A. Waksman in medicine. Einstein and Fermi were recognized for their pioneering work in atomic energy. Waksman is remembered for developing streptomycin, a powerful antibiotic that proved useful in treating tuberculosis and other diseases.

In literature, such writers as Boris Pasternak and Saul Bellow have received the Nobel Prize. In the area of peace, Jewish prize winners have included Henry Kissinger, who served in the administration of President Richard M. Nixon, and Elie Wiesel, a writer who survived several Nazi extermination camps. In Israel, Yitzhak Rabin and Shimon Peres, both of whom served as that nation's prime minister, were recognized for their efforts to achieve peace in the Middle East.

Music and Entertainment

Jews have more than distinguished themselves in the entertainment world. Beginning with Felix Mendelssohn (the *Wedding March*) in the early 19th century, they have produced some of the world's greatest musical artists. Numbered

among these are George Gershwin, Oscar Hammerstein, and Irving Berlin (songwriters and composers); Leonard Bernstein and Arthur Fiedler (conductors); Artur Rubinstein and Vladimir Horowitz (pianists); Al Jolson, Bette Midler, and Barbara Streisand

(singers); Yitzhak Perlman (violinist); and Beverly Sills (opera). Many more could be mentioned. Those listed include only some of the best known.

Jewish actors are numerous, but you wouldn't know them by their given names because many have changed to stage or screen names. Woody Allen, for example, is really Allen Koenigsberg. Jerry Lewis is Joseph Levitch, Lauren Bacall is Bette Perske, and Tony Curtis was Bernard Schwartz. Familiar with the Three Stooges of yesteryear? Moe was Moses Horwitz, Curly was Jerome Horwitz, and Shemp was Shemp Horwitz. And the list goes on.

Art and Literature

One of the most famous of Jewish painters is Marc Chagall. His paintings are noted for their dreamlike quality. In addition to those writers previously mentioned, an earlier Jewish writer who won wide acclaim was Sholom Aleichem (pen name of Sholom Rabinowitz). He wrote about Jewish life in the small towns

Albert Einstein (left), George Gershwin (center), and Marc Chagall (right) made significant contributions to the arts and sciences.

Words to remember:

monotheism
polytheism

ethical
monotheism

ethics
Mosaic Law

and villages of Eastern Europe. Other writers of note include Emma Lazarus, whose poem *The New Colossus* is inscribed on a plaque at the bottom of the Statue of Liberty, and Herman Wouk, whose novels about World War II have been made into hit movies. One of Wouk's more popular novels was *The Caine Mutiny*.

Sports

Jewish athletes have excelled in the world of sports. Again, we will mention only a few. In baseball, Hank Greenberg starred for the Detroit Tigers in the 1930s and 1940s, and Sandy Koufax was a great left-handed pitcher for the Los Angeles Dodgers several decades later. In football, Sid Luckman was a star quarterback at Columbia University and later won fame with the professional Chicago Bears.

Professional basketball has had its share of outstanding Jewish players and coaches. Players include the likes of Nat Homan of the Boston Celtics and Adolph Schayes of the old Syracuse Nationals. Two famous Jewish coaches are Red Holtzman of the New York Knickerbockers and Red Auerbach of the Boston Celtics.

Several Jewish swimmers have made names for themselves in the Olympics. One is Mark Spitz, who won seven gold medals at the 1972 Olympics. Almost 50 years earlier, Johnny Weissmuller won five gold medals during the 1920s. Weissmuller later achieved even greater fame in the 1930s when he played Tarzan in motion pictures.

Outstanding Jews mentioned in this chapter represent only a few who have achieved fame and made notable contributions to society. With a minimum of research, you can find and read about many others.

Sandy Koufax (above left) and Emma Lazarus (above right).

Section Review:

1. Name any 3 Jews who have achieved fame in the fields of music and entertainment.
2. How is poet Emma Lazarus connected with the Statue of Liberty?
3. Name three Jews who have been awarded the Nobel Prize?

For Further Thought:

1. Which contribution of the early Hebrews do you consider the most important? Why?
2. Research and write a report on one of the famous Jews mentioned in this chapter.
3. Contemplate the contributions European Jews might have made had it not been for the Holocaust. What percent of Jewish intellectuals and artists do you think might have perished in the extermination camps?
4. Explain the statement "Christianity is sometimes referred to as the *daughter of Judaism*."

TEST

NAME: _____

Circle the correct answer.

1. *He is considered to be the "Father of the Hebrews."*
   a. Moses   **b.** Abraham   **c.** Jeremiah

2. *The flight of the ancient Israelites (Hebrews) from Egypt is referred to as the*
   a. Exodus   **b.** Pentateuch   **c.** Babylonian Captivity

3. *The great Temple of Jerusalem was built in the 10th century B.C. by King*
   a. David   **b.** Saul   **c.** Solomon

4. *The Hebrew prophets differed from soothsayers in that they*
   a. only predicted the future.
   b. warned the Hebrews of what might happen to them if they disobeyed God.
   c. were all political advisors to kings.

5. *Jews living in exile, or not in Israel, are said to be living in the*
   a. Diaspora   **b.** Messianic Era   **c.** Exodus

6. *Organized massacres of a people such as the Jews are called*
   a. ghettos   **b.** pogroms   **c.** assassinations

7. *The goal of the Zionist Movement was to*
   a. convert people of other faiths to Judaism.
   b. militarily defeat the Arabs in the Middle East.
   c. establish a homeland for the Jews in Palestine.

8. *The Holocaust was a deliberate attempt on the part of this nation to exterminate the Jews of Europe.*
   a. Czarist Russia   **b.** Nazi Germany   **c.** Poland

9. *The nation of Israel was established*
   a. in the late 1800s.
   b. in 1948.
   c. shortly after World War I.

10. *Most Jews believe Jesus to be*
    a. the Messiah.
    b. a great teacher.
    c. God himself.

11. *The cabinet in a synagogue where the Torah scrolls are kept is called the*
    a. Ark.
    b. bimah.
    c. Ner Tamid.

12. *The spiritual leader of a synagogue has the title of*
    a. cantor.   **b.** pastor.   **c.** rabbi.

13. *The service in an Orthodox Jewish synagogue is conducted in*
    a. the vernacular.   **b.** Greek.   **c.** Hebrew.

14. *Mitzvot are*
    a. commandments Jews are expected to follow.
    b. palm branches used in the celebration of Sukkot.
    c. special prayers recited at Jewish funerals.

15. *Foods that are deemed proper for Jews to eat are referred to as*
    a. treyf.   **b.** kosher.   **c.** organic.

16. *For a Jewish boy and girl, Bar Mitzvah and Bat Mitzvah signify*
    a. the passage from childhood to adulthood.
    b. their total commitment to the Jewish faith.
    c. their vow to convert others to Judaism.

17. *Which branch of Judaism stresses strict adherence to traditional beliefs and customs?*
    a. Orthodox   **b.** Reform   **c.** Conservative

18. *The Jewish Holiday referred to as the Day of Atonement is*
    a. Rosh Hashanah.   **b.** Purim.   **c.** Yom Kippur.

19. *The Jewish holiday known as the Festival of Lights is*
    a. Pesach.   **b.** Sukkot.   **c.** Hanukkah.

20. *Monotheism is the belief in*
    a. one god.   **b.** no gods.   **c.** many gods.

SHORT ANSWER

1. *What covenant is God said to have made with Abraham?*

_____

_____

_____

2. *List any 3 basic beliefs shared by all Jews.*

_____

_____

_____

3. *How does Judaism differ from Christianity, a religion that sprang from it?*

_____

_____

_____

ANSWER KEY

Page 3
1. A tribe is a group of people descended from a common ancestor.
2. Abraham moved to the city of Haran. They moved because they needed water and grass for their flocks.
3. The covenant with God stated that as long as the Hebrews obeyed him and carried out his will, they would be his chosen people.
4. Canaan was a land situated between the Mediterranean Sea, the Arabian Desert, Egypt, and Mesopotamia.

Page 4
1. Abraham smashed the idols because he had come to believe in only one god.
2. God ordered Abraham to sacrifice his son to test Abraham's faith.
3. Answers will vary. Most students will write that Abraham's willingness to sacrifice his son proved that he was willing to obey God in all things.

Page 6
1. The Pentateuch consists of the first five books of the Bible.
2. God instructed Moses to return to Egypt and lead the Israelites out of captivity.
3. The term Passover goes back to the Angel of Death "passing over" the houses of the Israelites and sparing their first-born children.
4. The Pharaoh decided to set the Israelites free when his own son was taken from him by the Angel of Death.

Page 7
1. The Israelites' flight from Egypt is referred to as "The Exodus."
2. Moses received the Ten Commandments on top of Mount Sinai.
3. God condemned the Israelites to wander in the wilderness for 40 years.

Page 8
1. The Israelites were ruled by officials called judges.
2. The capital was established at Jerusalem by King David.
3. Solomon's extravagance made Israel ripe for revolt.

Page 9
1. The Fertile Crescent was an area that extended from the eastern end of the Mediterranean Sea to the Persian Gulf.
2. They became known as the Ten Lost Tribes after the Assyrians overran them and carried them away into captivity.
3. The Chaldeans conquered the Kingdom of Judah.
4. The modern nation of Israel was established in 1948.

Pages 11

1. Prophets were different from soothsayers in that they did not so much predict the future, but warned the Israelites what would happen to them if they disobeyed God.
2. The Assyrians conquered the kingdom of Israel.
3. Micah predicted Judah's downfall more than a hundred years before it occurred.
4. King Nebuchadnezzar conquered Jerusalem.
5. It is believed Malachi was the last of the prophets.

Page 13

1. The Diaspora refers to Jews living in exile.
2. Islam
3. Pope Urban II called the First Crusade to retake the Holy Land from the Muslims.
4. Many of the Jewish inhabitants were slaughtered by the Crusaders.

Pages 14

1. Among the accusations were charges that Jews sacrificed Christian children to Yahweh, that they poisoned Christian wells, that their women were sorceresses, and that they used Christian blood as medicine and to make unleavened bread.
2. Pope Innocent III decreed that Jews had to dress differently from other people.
3. Pogroms are organized massacres of people.
4. Ghettos are parts of cities where certain groups are forced to live in overcrowded conditions. They were established to segregate Jews from everyone else.

1. The Moors (Muslims) ruled Spain during much of the Middle Ages.
2. Jews in Spain lived in comfort and security.
3. The American and French Revolutions resulted in peace and tolerance for Jews throughout most of Europe.

Page 15

1. Frequent pogroms caused many Russian Jews to immigrate to the United States.
2. Golda Meir became the prime minister of Israel in 1969.
3. The goal of the Zionist Movement was the establishment of a homeland for Jews.
4. The Balfour Declaration was issued by Great Britain stating its support of a Jewish homeland in Palestine. It created tension between Jews and Arabs because Britain had made the same promise to the Arabs.

Page 16

1. The Holocaust was a deliberate attempt by Nazi Germany to exterminate the Jews of Europe.
2. At least 6 million Jews were exterminated.
3. The Jews were blamed primarily for all of Germany's economic problems.
4. The worst of the death camps were located in Poland.
5. The Final Solution was the Nazis' plan to exterminate the Jews in gas chambers.

Page 17

1. Israel became an independent nation in 1948.
2. They were attacked by six Arab states.
3. Answers will vary.

Page 18
1. A Jew is a person who adheres to the religion of Judaism.
2. Jews call God Yahweh, or Jehovah.
3. Jews believe that God chose Abraham to be the leader of a great nation. In return, the Jews would have to obey him and follow his laws.
4. Most Jews see Jesus as a great teacher and storyteller.

Page 19
1. The Jewish place of worship is called the synagogue.
2. Ancient Hebrews believed the Ark contained the Ten Commandments.
3. No one knows for certain what happened to the original Ark of the Covenant.
4. The Torah scrolls are kept in the Ark.
5. Among other duties, the rabbi conducts services; helps Jews understand the Torah; decides questions of Jewish law; helps people with personal problems, and teaches Judaism to adult groups.
6. The cantor chants traditional Jewish songs and prayers.

Page 21
1. The Jewish Sabbath begins on Friday at sundown and continues until Saturday at sundown. It is called Shabbat.
2. Services in a Reform synagogue are conducted in the vernacular.
3. Yarmulke: the skullcap worn by Jewish men; tallit: prayer shawl worn by men; tefillin: two small boxes worn by Orthodox Jewish men that contain pieces of parchment on which are written selections from the Old Testament.
4. The Written Torah contains the first five books of the Old Testament.
5. The Torah is written on strips of parchment that are sewn together in a long scroll.

Page 21
1. Mitzvot are commandments listed in the Torah.
2. They are similar in that they state things Jews are expected to do.

Page 24
1. Traditional Jews feel that they are reminded of God's presence when they touch the mezuzah.
2. A challah is a loaf of specially baked bread that is prepared for the Shabbat meal.
3. The kiddush prayer is recited before the Shabbat meal begins. The havdalah is recited when the Shabbat ends on Saturday evening.
4. Kosher foods are foods that Jews are allowed to eat.
5. Jews may not eat the likes of pigs, rabbits, and shellfish.

Page 25
1. Jews believe the Brit Milah ceremony stems from a covenant Abraham made with God.
2. Both ceremonies signify the passage from childhood to adulthood. They occur at age 12 for a girl and age 13 for a boy.
3. Reform Jews make no distinction between girls and boys in the way the ceremonies are carried out.
4. The confirmation ceremony is a time when young people at the age of 16 publicly announce their dedication to Judaism.

Page 26
1. The Jews believe that God instructed them to marry and to have children.
2. The canopy is called a huppah.
3. A ketubah is a marriage contract that some couples agree to.
4. The stepping on the wineglass is to remind the married couple of two things: that they are not to forget the sufferings of the Jewish people in history and that they are to remember the destruction of the First and Second Temples in ancient times.
5. Some Conservative and Reform Jewish weddings are double-ring ceremonies.

Page 27
1. Jewish funerals are often held within 24 hours of the death of the deceased.
2. A Kaddish is a prayer of mourning.
3. A shiva is a week of deep mourning after the death of a loved one.
4. A son or daughter may mourn the loss of a parent for as long as a year.

Page 29
1. The term "Orthodox Jew" was first used in the early 19th century.
2. Joseph Karo was a Talmudic scholar who drew up the Shulhan Arukh for Jews to follow.
3. The kashrut is the strict dietary code followed by some Jews.
4. Foods considered to be treyf are those thought to be unclean, such as pork and shellfish.

Page 30
1. Reform Judaism began in what is now Germany.
2. Political revolutions in the 18th century led to changes in religious thinking as well.
3. The Messianic era refers to the belief in a perfect world characterized by equality, freedom, and brotherhood.

Page 30
1. Conservative Judaism was founded by Zechariah Frankel.
2. The basic difference between Conservative and Reform Jews is the way they look at Jewish law. Reform Jews do not agree that Jewish law is binding. Conservative Jews do, but believe it can be changed to conform to modern times.

Page 32
1. Rosh Hashanah and Yom Kippur cover ten days in which Jews engage in prayer and penitence for what they did wrong during the year.
2. Both take place during the month of Tishri.
3. A shofar is a hollowed ram's horn that is blown at the beginning of Rosh Hashanah and at the end of Yom Kippur.
4. They do this to wish everyone a sweet and pleasant year.
5. The Tashlikh is a ceremony in which Jews symbolically cast their sins into the water.
6. Yom Kippur is a day of atonement when Jews ask forgiveness for their sins.

Page 33
1. Jews celebrate Hanukkah in remembrance of the Maccabees' struggle for freedom from the Syrians.
2. The Syrian king had tried to force the Jews to worship Greek gods. He also

defiled the Temple by sacrificing a pig at the altar.

3. *Maccabee* is the Jewish word for "hammer," which was the nickname of Judah, who led the revolt against the Syrians.

4. *Hanukkah* is called the "Festival of Lights" because each night for eight nights candles are lit on a special menorah called a Hanukkiah.

Page 34

1. Jews build huts in their gardens as a reminder of how the Hebrews lived during their time of wandering in the wilderness.

2. The roof of a sukkah is made of leaves and branches from which is hung fruit and perhaps paper chains and candy.

3. A lulav is a palm branch with sprigs of willow and myrtle. An etrog is a citron, a fruit similar to a lemon.

4. Simchat Torah is the holy day when the last passage of the Torah is read in the synagogue.

Page 36

1. *Purim* is called the "Feast of Lots" because that is how Haman, the chief minister to the king of Persia, chose the day in which the Jews of Persia would be killed.

2. The purpose of greggors is to drown out all mention of Haman's name.

3. The word *Passover* comes from Moses telling the Hebrews in Egypt to smear the doorjambs of their houses with lamb's blood. That way, the Angel of Death would "pass over" the house and spare the first-born child.

4. Jews eat only unleavened bread in remembrance of their hurried flight from Egypt.

5. The story of the Passover and the Exodus from Egypt are told during the meal.

Page 38

1. Monotheism is the belief in one god. Polytheism is the belief in many gods.

2. Mosaic Law is made up of the Ten Commandments and laws developed during the time of the Judges.

3. Jews divide the Old Testament into the Torah, the Prophets, and the Writings.

Page 39

1. Answers will vary.

2. Her poem, *The New Colossus*, is inscribed on a plaque at the Statue of Liberty.

3. Answers will vary.

Test: Page 41
Multiple Choice:

1. b   2. a   3. c   4. b   5. a   6. b   7. c   8. b   9. b   10. b   11. a
12. c   13. c   14. a   15. b   16. a   17. a   18. c   19. c   20. a

Short Answer:

1. God told Abraham he would become the leader of a great nation and that the Hebrews would be God's chosen people if they obeyed God and followed his will.

2. Belief in one, universal god; God made a covenant with Abraham; belief in a Messiah; the words of the prophets are true; Moses was the greatest of the prophets; the dead will be resurrected.

3. Judaism does not accept Jesus as the son of God or as the Messiah, as Christians do.

BIBLIOGRAPHY

Will Durant, *The Age of Faith* (Simon and Schuster, New York, 1950).

Nicholas De Lange, *Introduction to Judaism* (Cambridge University Press, Cambridge, 2000).

Judith F. Fellner, *In the Jewish Tradition: A Year of Foods and Festivities* (Smithmark Publishers, Inc., New York, 1995).

Laura Greene, *I Am an Orthodox Jew* (Holt, Rinehart and Winston, New York, 1979).

Martha Morrison and Stephen F. Brown, *Judaism: World Religions* (Facts on File, New York, 1991).

Jose Patterson, *Angels, Prophets, Rabbis, and Kings from the Stories of the Jewish People* (Peter Bedrick Books, New York, 1991).

Sue Penny, *Discovering Religions: Judaism* (Raintree Steck-Vaughn Publishers, Austin, Texas,1997).

The Shengold Jewish Encyclopedia (Edited by Mordecai Schreiber. Rockville, Maryland, 1998).

Mordecai I. Soloff, *When the Jewish People Was Young* (Union of American Hebrew Congregations, New York, 1934).

Monica Stoppleman, *Beliefs and Cultures: Jewish* (Children's Press, Danbury, Connecticut,1996).

Michael Strassfeld, *The Jewish Holidays: A Guide and Commentary* (Harper & Row, Publishers, New York,1985).

INTERNET SITES

Beyond the Pale: The Middle Ages.
http:www.friends-partners.org/partners/beyond-the-pale/english/ob.html.

Judaism 101: What Do Jews Believe?
http:www.jewfaq.org/beliefs.htm

Torah Scribes: A Vanishing Breed.
http://www.s-t.com/daily/07-97/07-28-97/c02ho094.htm.